Contents

Acknowledgements 2

Introduction 3

1	"I'll never do an Ironman"	4
2	From Bolton to Hawaii	22
3	Spoilt brat	41
4	Transitions	58
5	Turbulent times	69
6	Covid, long Covid and Ironman UK	79
7	Training and race tips	93
8	The Big C	106
9	There is no place like home	129

Acknowledgements.

To Charlie for your incredible strength of character, care, kindness, positivity and support. For the hugs and hand holding.

To Andy for your wonderful care and support through my illness, surgery and ongoing recovery. For enjoying the good times and supporting me through the dark times. For all the race prep, transport, massages, mechanics and advice.

Huge thanks to everyone mentioned in this book. Particularly to Fabio, my wonderful surgeon and all the sarcoma team at the Queen Elizabeth hospital.

Thanks to the kind nurses named in the book for your hard work and care. To all my friends and family for your time and company, kindness and comforting words.

INTRODUCTION

It just didn't seem right. My Garmin watch informed me, as a 51-year-old Mum (albeit as a competing athlete) that I had a VO2 max reading of 76 and an average resting heart rate of 31. Yet, what it couldn't tell me was that I had a 19CM, 5KG cancer in my abdominal cavity. When I was diagnosed, I couldn't understand how this could be true with my fitness stats as they were.

This book summarises some important events in my life to date and what led me to Ironman racing. It covers setbacks and comebacks, my cancer journey and (with hope and prayer) my road to recovery.

As I am often asked for advice, I have also used this opportunity to offer tips on training, racing and as a separate topic, positive thinking, all of which I sincerely hope will help others.

Being in good health is obviously fundamental to good racing, and my 'numbers' had convinced me that I was in peak condition in 2022. Even on the day before I was diagnosed, I comforted myself with the thought, it obviously can't be cancer. You can't do a full Ironman with cancer. How wrong can you be?!

CHAPTER 1. "I'll never do an Ironman"

Ironman races are pretty extreme endurance events and a goal of many triathletes. The Ironman distances are - 3.8km open water swim, 180km bike and finally a 42km (full Marathon) run. The race itself is a relative minor part of the lifestyle choice which involves a great deal of sacrifice and dedication.

The book starts by explaining what led to my cancer diagnosis and then looks back to my childhood and how I went from a 1500m track runner to Ironman triathlete.

I wanted to write this book to set out to myself and others how I arrived at such a major moment in my life, how I reached my level of fitness and how it all came crashing down. Hopefully the book isn't too self-indulgent and anyone who does read it can gain something positive from it. If nothing else I have found the project hugely cathartic during an incredibly difficult period.

Training and racing have been an amazing and hugely important part of my life and perhaps the best thing about it all is the fitness it gave me and the comfort and peace of mind that I must be in good health to do what I do. Clearly my health wasn't as good as I thought and I doubt I will feel that level of assurance ever again. I am certain though, that my fitness has helped hugely with my recovery and is possibly one of the reasons I am still here today.

As mentioned in the introduction, my fitness stats were pretty rare, and more in line with a young athlete than a working middle-aged Mum.

For those of you who don't know – VO2 max is the maximum rate of oxygen your body is able to use during exercise. The greater your VO2 max, the more oxygen your body can consume and the more effective your body is at generating energy....for things like swimming, cycling and running.

On July 4th 2022, I raced Ironman UK in Bolton. This course is one of the toughest Ironman races on the circuit with around 8000ft climbing on the bike and over 1200ft on the run. The road surface is dangerous in places, strewn with potholes, there are sections of the course marked as disallowed for tri-bars (aero bars which are extensions to the handlebars) and of course there is the British weather to factor in. During this 2022 race, we had our fair share of rain and wind to add to the entertainment.

This was the sixth full Ironman race I had competed in, previously racing....

Switzerland 2003, Switzerland 2004, Bolton 2016

Hawaii 2016, Vichy 2018 and returning to Bolton in 2022.

Before turning to Ironman events, I had previously raced in the Great Britain age group team for sprint and Olympic distance triathlons as well as standard distance duathlon (10km run, 40km bike, 5km run) winning an age group bronze medal in the World Championships at the latter. At the time, I looked on the Ironman athletes with curiosity but always maintaining "I will never do an Ironman - that's crazy". Hmmmmm!....

I started racing longer distance events after meeting my (now) husband Andy, and certainly having a close companion racing these events inspired me.

In 2001, aged 30 I completed my first half Ironman. That's the kind of thing we did together when we first started "dating".

The event was in North Wales and was incredibly scenic and also pretty hilly. Despite lack of training or preparation and a night before on the Bacardi, the distance seemed to suit me. Finishing 3rd in my category, I was hooked....

Encouraged and inspired by Andy, 2003 was then my first experience at Full Ironman. We chose to race Ironman Switzerland, largely so we could enjoy the location and combine it with a holiday type trip. Training together and then driving through Europe to Zurich we were both very excited.

Sadly, after a nasty fall on the bike during a practice ride Andy was unable to start.

We had headed out to check the bike course a few days before the event. It was a perfect sunny day, 33 degrees with not a cloud in the sky and the scenery around Zurich was absolutely stunning. We enjoyed the lake and mountain views, a section of switch backs and a long slow climb at the far end of the bike route. Heading through some beautiful Swiss villages and then onto a downhill section, through some wooded areas and onto the steepest part of the descent, Andy in front.

Suddenly Andy's front wheel was wrenched to the right followed by his bike, as Andy continued straight down the hill at around 40mph. I slammed my brakes on and came to a stop just in front of the cause of his crash – Tram lines!

Tram lines are hated by many cyclists, particularly if they run at a diagonal on the road, wheels can get trapped in them, sending the cyclist flying through the air straight onto the tarmac, this is exactly what happened to Andy. Race day they are temporarily filled in, to make them safe for the riders but as we were a few days before the event they were left exposed and we hadn't seen the signs.

Quickly dismounting and running to Andy where he lay on the road, I found he was badly cut and bruised, but thankfully conscious. He had terrible gravel rash and pieces of gravel and dirt imbedded into his backside, thigh and knees.

Somehow, he managed to get back on his bike and we rode, very slowly, back to the hotel.

The bruising and inflammation were both horrendous by the time we reached the hotel and I was concerned that he should be in hospital and certainly seeking medical help. Andy (being slightly stubborn) would have none of it, claiming "If I go to hospital, you won't race so I'm not going. I'll clean it out myself." He then went into the shower and scrubbed his wounds clean! I definitely couldn't have inflicted that sort of pain on myself and it said so much for how he felt about my racing.

The following days leading up to race day, Andy walked around with his wounds on show, trying to aid recovery with fresh air, with maybe even some slight hope he may still compete. It probably wasn't the best idea given how deep some of the gashes were but he still stubbornly refused medical help, despite my protestations that he should go to hospital.

I was so touched by his determination to ensure I was on that start line, despite his clear discomfort and pain, but was also very concerned for him.

Other competitors would see his wounds and wince, guessing what had happened and probably feeling relieved it wasn't them. It was very upsetting to see Andy in so much pain and accepting that for him, the race was over before it had even started. It obviously also took the edge off the excitement for my first Ironman. Having trained together so well and with such dedication, it seemed so cruel to have it snatched away for him.

By race day though Andy had encouraged me and was so positive that I still managed to stand on the start line and feel a fizz of excitement return.

The swims back then were mostly mass starts so I lined up with the other competitors on the lakeside beach and when the Claxon sounded, 2500 athletes stormed into the water. It made for some great pictures but was more of a fight than a swim for the first quarter mile. Despite the mayhem, I managed to have a good swim and decent transition, but as so often happens with these longer races, there was a problem on the bike.

Even with half Ironman, I seem to be able to train well on the bike for months and ensure all the necessary maintenance checks are carried out but on race day, often have "a technical", it's so frustrating. On this my very first Ironman event, it was inevitable; I punctured and lost a lot of time, eventually waiting for the official help wagon to come to my rescue with a replacement inner tube. The two carried in my saddlebag would not inflate. We later discovered there was a faulty batch with the brand we had used so really, on this occasion it wasn't entirely my fault. I finished the bike leg and despite a hugely tiring marathon run, was overjoyed to eventually finish and hear for the first time ever announced over the commentator speaker, "SAMANTHA KENNEDY – CONGRATULATIONS, YOU ARE NOW AN IRONMAN!!"

For this trip, we stayed in a very basic hotel but in a wonderful location and enjoyed a holiday around Zurich after the event, returning to normal life after what seemed like months thinking about nothing except Ironman.

The shops in Zurich helped, they were incredible. One day we were walking around the shops, having spent most days lazing by the lake or walking in the countryside. I spotted a Versace dress in one of the windows and stopped to look. The shop owner came out and tried to persuade me to try it on, she really was very insistent.... It was £2000 and I had my shorts and muddy trainers on, clomping around.

I didn't try the dress on but it was nice to be asked and great fun to window shop in a city where everyone was so friendly.

Andy – out of Ironman Switzerland 2003

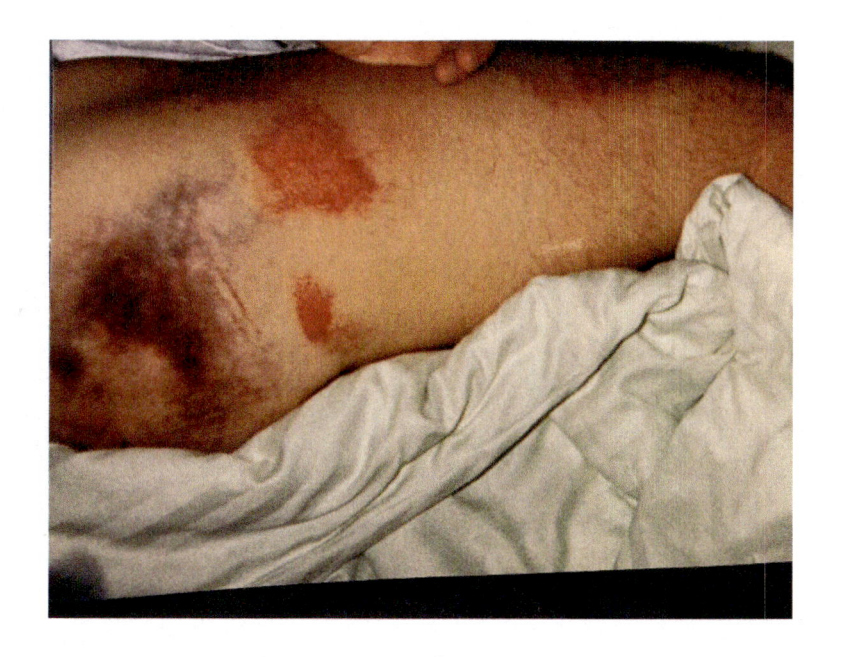

Switzerland IM race start – My first ever

Racing up heart break hill Ironman Switzerland 2003

That 2003 event changed my life, I loved my new found sport, and as Andy had experienced such a disastrous trip, we were determined to return the following year and both race Ironman Switzerland in 2004.

In the run up to the second attempt, we shared some great times training together, heading to the Cotswolds water park on a Saturday morning for a swim in the lake followed by a bike around the Cotswold villages, sometimes followed by a run too…. And always a coffee and cake afterwards of course. Often friends would come and join us and add to the entertainment, which always ensured these normally hard training sessions were nothing but wonderful fun.

Many training sessions are monotonous or fade from memory by tea time, but others become ingrained in the mind, especially, the tougher sessions. I can still picture today, cycling through the winter of 2003/2004 with the Beacon cycling club, every Sunday morning. Some days we would ride through howling wind and torrential rain, dodging huge puddles on muddy lanes and hunching against the spray of the road as people flew by in their warm, dry cars.

There are many memorable track sessions, running mile reps in similar conditions in the pitch black. We would be the only ones on the track, no-one else was crazy enough. We absolutely refused to miss a single session. Mid-week after work we ran and swam together. We trained in some terrible weather conditions, so determined that BOTH of us would be on the start line for Ironman Switzerland 2004.

Andy was probably the fittest he has ever been but possibly we both over trained. We were so determined to do well that we didn't respect the rest required and just did too much. We arrived in Zurich for the second attempt, fatigued and both carrying niggles, having trained too many miles on the bike, too many miles running, too intensely and with too short a taper.

Hobbling around the run, race day, I was gutted to notice Andy in the crowd. He had pulled up on the run and dropped out. I still think he should have carried on. He was in the shape of his life and was going so well but his calf had given up on him in the second part of the run.

Andy was stood cheering with my Mum and Dad who had come to watch this race. They had never seen Ironman before, let alone watched their daughter compete in one. They thoroughly enjoyed the experience.

Both Mum and Dad were so much more adventurous than us, holidaying in glamourous locations such as Galapagos, South Africa, and even a hike to Everest base camp to name just a few of their trips. I have always loved and admired this side of my parents' personalities.

During this second trip to Zurich, prior to the race, Andy and I were out driving to registration and we stopped to check out a beautiful river. Looking right we couldn't believe what we were seeing... My Mum and Dad back packing down a path at the side of the river, fresh from the airport and a lengthy train journey. We had a lovely holiday with them but before the race I said to Mum .... "I hope you enjoy the experience of watching this race Mum because I am never, ever, ever doing another Ironman."

I can't remember if it was a day or possibly two after the race, when I said to Andy "I wonder what the dates will be for next year?"

This is what Ironman does to you, it kicks you until you can't move, then coaxes you back the following year with the promise that the next one might be easier. It never is.

We would not be returning to Switzerland the following year; we had other plans. Although we met through our shared enjoyment of triathlons, it was clear that we had more in common than just that and inevitably Andy and I married in March 2005.

We didn't have a great deal of money (spending much of it on racing) and as it was second marriages for us both, we did everything on a budget.

The wedding day was kept very low key, having only close friends and immediate family for a meal, followed by relaxed drinks with more friends in the evening. Family took the photographs, providing us with some great shots. Tying a ribbon around Dad's car, we had our official wedding carriage. We had a small cake and minimal flowers. My dress (NOT Versace!) cost under five hundred pounds; less than both Andy's suit and my Mums outfit, but I think they were just relieved I wasn't in trainers. We did the entire event for under five thousand pounds, which included our honeymoon, a week in Fuerteventura – not racing!

Despite the lack of luxury and expense, it was relaxed and exactly what we wanted. Happily, everyone said it was a great day and enjoyed themselves which was good enough for us.

Andy is one of eight. When I learned this my first question was "Oh are you catholic? And me."

Andy is not catholic. He just has a big family and when I married him, I married into the whole Boswell clan. On the day of our wedding, as soon as the service finished his lovely Mum gave me a hug and said "Welcome to the family."

Andy's Mum was the matriarch of the Boswell family and everyone always gravitated towards her. Sadly, she is no longer with us but I have such fond memories of her. She often had a cheeky giggle or knowing smile and for years, every Saturday most of the family would squash into her front room and spend a couple of hours mocking and hurling abuse at each other (in a very loving way of course). Really precious memories of a lovely lady.

A few days after the wedding, we took our honeymoon in Fuerteventura, where we then discovered we actually had something far more exciting than racing to look forward to. I felt a little off, as though suffering with a temperature and was incredibly tired. We bought a test and discovered the wonderful news... I was pregnant.

We were both thrilled and some months later, we were lucky enough to have our dreams come true, giving birth to our son Charlie in December 2005. Obviously, the best thing we have ever done and will always be my proudest achievement. It was clear from the start we had created a beautiful soul.

Charlie, of course, became my priority and I changed my whole routine for him, choosing to work three days a week and spend most of my time with him. I didn't train or race for months and cherished the time where he was so tiny.

Charlie and I shared wonderful times together. We met with friends, attending a village toddler group and took lots of walks at local parks. We went swimming twice a week. He was like a little fish before he was even one. Just as my Dad had for me, I taught Charlie to swim.

I loved swimming as a child, Saturday morning with my Dad at the local pool. They were the only swimming lessons I have ever needed, certainly from a safety point of view. It was the same for Charlie who learned by just enjoying the water and then watching his Mum. Though somehow his technique is far superior to mine. It's one less thing to worry about as a Mum, knowing my boy can swim.

Those early years passed quickly and when Charlie started school, I had a little more time to myself so, persuaded by a friend (Tony), joined a local cycling club and started training again. There was no real ambition to return to Ironman at this stage, just to return to some sort of fitness and race some shorter events.

The club was The Saracen Road Cycling club. Many members commented, "Oh great, we are glad you have joined, you have brought the average age of the club right down". Most of the members were retired with some over seventy. They were a lovely group and the right pace for me at the time, very much looking after me and giving me advice. "Change down a gear Sam" was often shouted along with "Get out of that big ring" or "Come on slow coach" whenever we hit a descent, or a junction, or mud or a bend!

The group would meet and pre ride discussion would start along the lines of "How is your knee?" "What's the latest on your hip?" or "How's your prostrate problem" etc etc, but as I say they were a good pace for me, I had to work hard to stay with some of them and many had been very strong riders at a high level in their day and some were still racing in their age categories.

Having limited time actually worked quite well for me. I couldn't put anything off until tomorrow because there was always something else to do, with Charlie to care for and entertain or work to attend. So I either trained when the chance occurred or sacrificed the session... I pretty much always chose to do the session.

After a couple of years, slowly becoming fitter and keener, a previous member re-joined and I was introduced to him. Mike (or Mick to his cycling friends) wanted to return to racing and time trialling and was constantly criticised (in a friendly way) for "half wheeling" and pushing the pace. I quite liked it. So eventually we would ride on our own as fast as we could.

Mick soon returned to racing and time trialling and really helped my cycling improve… it had to if I wanted to continue to ride with him. There was then several years riding with Mick and my cycling continued to improve. The rides with him were often not very enjoyable, purely down to the fact they were always hard, but they certainly helped me improve.

So as Charlie grew and started school, and my appetite for pushing myself on the bike and on longer runs came back, I slowly ventured back into the world of competitive endurance racing.

ER 2. From Bolton to Hawaii.

During the years after having Charlie and when he first started school, I raced a number of times for Great Britain over the shorter distances - sprint, standard and also duathlon (run-bike-run). These are much more attainable distances to train for with a young child but what are still considered endurance events with even the "sprint" taking around an hour.

Despite enjoying and performing reasonably well at these events, (winning Bronze at the Duathlon World championships) I never felt these shorter distances were my strength and couldn't stop thinking about the longer courses and wondering about the elusive Hawaii Ironman. Hawaii is the location of the Ironman world championships, it's where the sport was born and the most prestigious event on the Ironman race calendar.

By 2016, when Charlie was ten, I felt the time was right to race Ironman again. I had a great twelve months around this time as an age group athlete, winning the National championships at both sprint and standard distance and becoming the British champion in the middle distance (half ironman distance) in a time of 4hrs45 minutes, a personal best that still stands for me today. Thrilled with these wins, the results encouraged me to dive back into Ironman training and racing.

The Ironman we selected for ease of logistics and cost was Ironman UK. Training went well, possibly due to factoring some rest periods into my training, despite my constant desire to train, train and train some more.

Andy had given up triathlons at this point to pursue other interests but was very supportive to me, acting as my massage therapist, driver and bike mechanic. Sometimes after returning from a long, hard ride, soaked and bitterly cold, I would head straight to the shower, finding later that my bike had magically cleaned itself.

As the day of Ironman UK dawned, Andy and Charlie were my official support crew. It must have been very hard for the pair of them, particularly Andy. He would drive me there, drive all around the event, registering, drive to rack the bike at T1 (transition 1, swim to bike), leaving run kit at T2 (bike to run) in a totally different location and ensure I was at the start line in plenty of time, meaning I could concentrate on myself and focus on the race. All this he did, while looking after a ten-year-old boy bursting with energy. Perhaps the easier job was hopping off for a swim, bike, run for the day.

Ironman UK 2016 went well. After a good strong swim, there were only a few, minor hitches on the bike this time; my drink bottle came flying off during a section of terrible road surface near the start. I chose to jump off and run back for the bottle, not wanting to skip my vital hydration. Then, the first time up Sheep house lane (quite a well-known climb on the course), my saddlebag containing all my spares and tools rattled free over a cattle grid. Knowing my luck with punctures, I pulled over and ran back to retrieve that too.

Running back to fetch things doesn't quite give a professional image of a well-trained Ironman athlete, but strange things always happen on these long events, and you just have to react to these minor issues as you see best.

Retrieving my saddle bag, it was a lot harder to get going again on such a steep hill from a stationary position but in the end, a good ride meant finishing the bike leg fastest in my age, despite the two short stops. Although tired towards the end of the run, where I felt I should have gone better, I conceded it was still a decent run and all in all, it meant taking first place in my age category.

We were over the moon to hear this and it meant winning my slot to Hawaii. The three of us were very emotional and incredibly excited, all my training and hard work had paid off, we were off to the Ironman world championships and I was going to race in Hawaii.

Kona - Ironman Hawaii. The location where Ironman started and a race I had read so much about. For all the qualifying events, including Bolton, only one slot per age category was allocated for the women so only a win would guarantee qualification.

Standing lakeside at the Ironman UK race start, I thought there might be a chance of winning but athletes travel from all over the world to try and qualify and my age group had the highest number of women racing for that one spot, so it was clear it would be tough. Many of the top women have coaches and some are full time athletes, unlike myself who was a completely self-coached, working Mum.

Winning Ironman UK was definitely a team effort though, with Charlie and Andy both helping and cheering all day long. Charlie proved to be my magic weapon on the day, shouting louder than anyone "Come on Mum put your back into it". That raised a laugh from me and the surrounding athletes, and lifted my spirits just when it was needed. Support like that from your loved ones just helps you run a little longer and forget the pain for a short time.

It was such an amazing feeling when we realised, I had the win and very surreal standing on the podium in first place then signing my name to accept my Hawaii slot, which would be in October that year, just three months later.

Those three months in between races were a tricky balance between recovery and picking the training back up for a second peak whilst taking precautions not to fall into bad habits and over training.

Hawaii was then my fourth full Ironman and looking back, we all feel it was the best place we have ever been, we all have so many wonderful memories of the trip.

Getting there was nothing short of a disaster though. We had booked with Expedia and naively thought that if the connecting flight times only allowed around 3 hours between flights, then that should be fine. Both Andy and I had to book time off work for the trip so with limited holidays we couldn't go as long as we wanted and the trip including all travel was to be completed in 9 days.

We also had to take Charlie out of school for that period but his head teacher was very understanding, recognising it would be a great experience for him.

The day before we flew out, we spent a lovely evening at a Heathrow hotel ready for the flight the next morning. No problems there and we set off in high spirits. We flew from Heathrow to Seattle but unfortunately then hit a few problems. The connecting flight time clearly didn't allow enough time between the two flights.

Security had been tightened immensely over recent years and as we were exiting the first flight and waiting to clear one of the many security measures, panic started to set in about missing the next flight – which sure enough we did.

My kit didn't though! Off my bike and race kit went along with all our cases to Kona, Hawaii, whilst we were stranded in Seattle airport.

It then went from bad to worse. Panicking, we ran round to a helpdesk only to be told that the next flight from Seattle would have put us in Hawaii the day after the race. I was distraught at this stage. Andy must have been really worried too but he didn't show it and calmly found another help desk and amazingly sorted it all out.

We were to stay in a Double Tree hotel at the airport and fly the next day to Los Angeles with then a seven hour wait until the flight from Los Angeles to Kona. The hotel was pleasant and we were well looked after, Charlie falling asleep as soon as we arrived at our room, he was so exhausted. We had no other clothes as they were all enroute to Hawaii so had to put our sweaty clothes on the next day to travel in, which was not pleasant for any of us. The day before, we had been that family, sprinting to the airport gate just as the ever so charming and helpful lady on the gate gave us a sweet smile as she closed the door.

The following morning though we had plenty of time and boarded our flight from Seattle to LA and then onto Kona, Hawaii.

When we finally arrived at Kona airport, two days after we were scheduled, it was the Tuesday evening. The race was that Saturday so nowhere near enough time to acclimatise and to adjust to the time difference and jet-lag. We were also very stressed wondering where our cases and more importantly where my bike had ended up and even uncertain if it had been sent back to the UK or Seattle, given that we were nowhere to be seen.

We walked out the Kona airport, which is little more than a thatched hut with me almost in tears, only to be greeted by a young Hawaiian… "You must be the Boswells?" "I have your bike and cases here ready for you, don't worry it's all fine".

We all hugged this wonderful man. From then on, the trip was so chilled and calm it was surreal; particularly as there was another Ironman to do in four days' time, with a few little matters like acclimatising, assembling the bike, viewing the course, registering and transitions to sort.

Somehow, we seemed to fit it all in and still have some down time in the days running up to the race. Swimming with turtles and some of the best snorkelling in the world. It's fair to say it was a little different to Bolton. The hotel was fantastic and everyone we met was lovely and helpful and so calm and chilled, you couldn't help but adopt the same attitude.

The Hawaii Ironman event is so impressive and is set up to look after all the athletes and make them feel special, all having qualified in similar races and facing that tough process with such limited slots. Being part of that buzz was both incredibly exciting but also nerve racking.

Sponsors walked around and would notice your athlete wrist band and hand out free gifts – watches, beach towels, bags, nutrition and T-shirts all being thrust our way. So many wonderful volunteers helping with registration and transition set up. I had never known anything like it.

Come race morning, feeling so very nervous but also incredibly excited we made our way down to the race area, Andy driving. So early it was still dark and staying a little way out from the race site, eerily quiet. Surprisingly I had managed a few hours' sleep that night, but it was a very early start as always and leaving around 3am felt like the middle of the night.

A short drive and we arrived at the race location, which illuminated the sky with spot lights and filled the air with music. I hugged Andy and Charie, kissed them goodbye and headed over to body marking where my race number was applied using a temporary tattoo. Unusually all athletes are weighed so weight recorded, I nervously made my way over to transition to check the bike and add hydration and fuel.

It seemed like forever to wait until the age group athletes could enter the water to make our way to the start, by which time I had watched the sunrise and stood watching the swell of the Pacific Ocean, it's the bluest sea I have ever seen…. And also, a number of reality checks as several trips to the porta-loos were called for.

At last, all female age-group athletes were given the signal to head out to the start buoys and await the cannon fire to signal the race start. Treading water and looking down, all sorts of fish could be seen, oblivious to the huge mass of nerves above them and even a turtle swimming beneath the hundreds of legs kicking, anxiously waiting.

Enjoying the sites and feeling more relaxed, there was suddenly a huge BOOM! The cannon had fired and we were off. A huge surge of adrenaline flooded my body and I must have grinned the entire way through the swim – if that is even possible.

Continuing to savour the sight of fish swimming below us as we ventured deeper and deeper, until eventually all that could be seen was the blue being reflected back. I stopped looking then, having had several weird dreams about sharks in the lead up to the race. As always swimming wide, though it means swimming a little further and not getting a drag from the crowd; it also means I'm more likely to keep my goggles in place and not get kicked or collided into. When younger and we all started together, men and women, all ages, I was less afraid but age has brought more caution of being involved in the washing machine effect of a mass start.

The swim seemed to end quickly and exiting from the water feeling fresh and comfortable, I was pleased the training had been spot on, for that element at least.

BUT, earlier on, before the race had even started, I had made a silly error. The nerves and awe of the event I had read so much about perhaps was a contributing factor. It was such a novelty having my own helper in transition and I gratefully allowed one of the lovely volunteers to pump up my tyres, also using his own pump rather than my known track pump, carried around with me all morning. Why?!

I'm not sure if too much pressure was used or if I was just unfortunate (we will never know) but after a great swim and first few miles on the bike thinking, hey up I could be on for a good day here... BANG! The sound no cyclist wants to hear. My rear tyre exploded.

"Not again!" I screamed to myself. Although the fitness and strength were there to ride a bike well, I never took the time to learn much about the mechanics or how best to get the bike going again if things went wrong, and yes, admittedly, I was not very proficient, to say the least at changing an inner tube. Clearly, this would have been a good thing to practice more; but I didn't. Now it was coming back to bite me.

To save time (HA!) and weight, I had thought a good system in-case of a puncture, would be to use liquid latex as a sealant along with gas canisters to inflate the tyres. After the bang, when it dawned on me that, yes, it came from my rear tyre, I initially tried to stay calm but as more and more women came past me, stood by the roadside, the panic started to rise. I then emptied latex all over the road, spraying it white and the gas canister into the humid Hawaiian air. At one stage after trying my second spare inner tube and second canister, my bike was turned in anger and frustration to head back into town and withdraw.

Stopping everything for a moment and trying to think calmly through the tears. Muttering to myself

"How do I even get back into town?" "How do I contact Andy? He thinks I am still on the course and has returned to the hotel" and "I have no dry kit to wear if I do head back." Thankfully I talked myself round.

Helped by my childhood running coach Keith and his voice in my head, who would not have been happy with a defeatist attitude and also thinking…How could I ever wear my Ironman World champs finishers T-shirt? I couldn't. One final attempt at getting some air in my third inner tube using an old emergency pump and, managing to get a few puffs of air in the tyre, I turned the bike back away from town, remounted and carried on.

The remainder of the 112-mile bike was then completed on a very soft rear tyre, estimating around 45psi where as I would normally race on around 100. Annoyingly, the puncture happened at mile 8 so there was a long, long way to go and it killed my legs plus of course my head was gone. I struggled to enjoy much of the remaining 104 miles of the bike course, knowing full well as people cheered, I should have been well ahead of where I was positioned and wanted to shout this to everyone on the course, athletes and spectators.

That feeling continued for the entire rest of the bike course and handing a volunteer my bike heading into the bike to run transition (T2) I muttered to him

"Just throw it away, I never want to see the thing again."

The volunteer replied with a chuckle "You will want it back 5 miles into the run" My legs were even more battered than normal, riding on a semi-inflated tyre so, he wasn't wrong.

Andy and I had spoken about Hawaii numerous times and agreed that if I ever made it to Hawaii, I would make it my last full Ironman and switch back to half distance so we would have more time together and less pressure on the races. Perhaps some holidays without dragging a bike and race kit around? So, during the run my main thoughts were, my legs are shot thanks to the puncture disaster and this is my last ever Ironman, what a way to go out!

The run on the Ironman is of course always tough but the heat and humidity on top of my (more than normal) tired bike legs made the run seem a lot longer and harder than normal. The heat reflects back off the road and back from the larva. It was like no heat I have raced in before.

I finished the race in a reasonable time and position but still fixated on what happened on the bike and the whole heap of time lost there. It was nowhere near what I felt it should have and could have been.

Shouted on by Andy and Charlie as always, they were over the moon to be cheering me on down that red carpet. Calling out to them about the puncture and explaining it all in tears at the end to which Andy replied… "Well. We just have to come back and do it all again then."

I couldn't have loved Andy more at that point, all the disappointment vanished and I proudly wore my finishers T-shirt and looked at the trip as a learning experience. One of the many wonderful things about this sport is years and years down the line, and all those races under my belt and I am still learning - and still have a lot to learn.

The winner of our age-group, a Brit I hasten to add, was very friendly and approachable so asking her advice about pressure and tyre choice, her first words in her reply were "Please God, tell me you didn't allow a random helper to pump up your tyres with a random pump on race day!?!?."

Yep afraid I did.

The days following the Hawaii Ironman, we had some wonderful, unforgettable times as a family, including a snorkel trip to Captain Cooks point where we saw dolphins, flying fish, turtles and hundreds of other different, brightly coloured fish. Charlie loved the water and seeing such exotic wildlife. After dropping anchor, a way off shore and diving in, he was probably hugely embarrassed by me who had definitely shifted back into "Mum mode" calling out "Come back Charlie, that's too deep."

In Hawaii, the water is fairly shallow and then suddenly drops off very deep and ten-year-old Charlie kept swimming over this subterranean cliff edge so we had to swim after him time after time as he tested us in this very deep water, and it was very, very deep. I pictured all sorts so kept going after him as he laughed, enjoying his new game. It was a great day though, and one we will always cherish. There was a slide and diving board off the boat and Charlie encouraged me to join him on both as he went from one to the other and looped round and round again, tirelessly as only a ten-year-old can.

A memory we will remember as the stand out experience of the trip, was a night swim with Manta rays. A few days after the race, we took an organised boat tour and in pitch black we ventured out into the Pacific on a small boat, not far off the coast. A couple of floats with lights on are thrown in the water by the skipper, followed by anyone brave enough to see what is attracted. Charlie had been very keen but as the boat headed deeper, I could sense him wavering, (he wasn't the only one).

When it came time to enter the water Charlie said "I'm sorry I just can't do it." He was eager for us to still go ahead as was the skipper of the boat. Reluctantly we entered the water, leaving Charlie on board and held onto the float with others on the trip. We called out to Charlie telling him how amazing it was and that he would be fine but he wouldn't budge. "No, I'm OK Mum. I've got a hot chocolate now."

As we hung onto the float, the manta rays came and Andy and I couldn't believe we were there and experiencing these majestic animals swooping and dancing, hoovering up the plankton right in front of us. Only five minutes later, our heads down we both felt a shove.

"Budge over you two, let a little one in."

The young marine biologist on the boat had talked with Charlie and swam with him out to our float after persuading him to join us. It was the most magical experience and I don't think any of us will ever forget these wonderful precious memories.

Hawaii 2016

Race start location

Family day trip.

Hawaii Ironman run route.

CHAPTER 3. Spoilt brat

Re-visiting my childhood at this point to explain how I moved from one sport to the other and how sport has always suited my personality and lifestyle. My brother, Daniel and I had a good childhood with many happy memories. Mum and Dad always did their best for us. They would move to the best school catchment areas, pushing their own finances to allow us to live in these locations. Between them they would always make these houses wonderful homes. We were also fortunate enough to have two family holidays every year, and like most families in the late 70's these were nearly always in the UK. We spent many holidays in the Lake District, Eskdale being a favourite and Cornwall around Bedruthan Steps.

Often in the Lake District we would stay on a friendly farm and hire a caravan, Daniel and I would turn feral. Playing in the woods, building dams in the river and running around the farm and fields with the other feral children. We played hide and seek in the hay and there would always be a regular organised barn dance and barbeque. I don't remember spending any time inside the caravans on these holidays, it was all about being outside.

As a young teenager I would sulk, complaining "It's not fair! All my friends are off to Spain and Greece and they will have lovely tans. I'll just be dragged up another mountain in the rain or sat on a windy cold beach with a coat on."

In my adult years though as I look back, these Lake District holidays, full of exploration, adventures, rain and fun are some of the best holiday memories and of course we enjoy similar holidays as a family with our son in the UK now. Climbing Great Gable, Scafell Pike and, Helvellyn, via a tough route called Striding Edge and walking around the beautiful Stanley Ghyll waterfalls.

Our recent family trip to Scotland was also fun, (if cold and wet). We climbed Ben Nevis and visited Steall falls and spent a lot of time outside, in the rain. As well as walking the mountains, one of our favourite family holidays now is surfing in Woolacombe, Devon. We go at least once a year. We all have body boards and catching a wave all together is magical, something the rain cannot spoil. Thankfully Charlie already loves all these types of holidays.

Growing up, Dad was much stricter and more vocal than Mum and we often clashed. He dislikes hugging. Hates it! But if Mum ever shouted at me, or really just gave me "a look" I knew I had really messed up, often though she was the peace keeper between Dad and I.

Dad was also the kind that worked really hard and for long hours. He has such an amazing work ethic and strong moral beliefs and I'm so proud of him for that. He must have often been tired when I was younger, with the hours he worked and the miles he covered, often driving over a thousand miles Monday to Friday. He would return home at the end of the day, to me bouncing off the walls, my younger, hyperactive self must have been a handful for both Mum and Dad. From around the age of six, my Dad would walk through the door, to be greeted by me begging him to come for a run. Even after his early starts for work, miles and miles of driving and sometimes a big business lunch, he would still get his trainers on and belch his way around the block for a run with me. Like most kids, I didn't appreciate his sacrifice at the time, but certainly do now.

He let me into a secret one day. He would sprint around the corner as we approached home, leaving me behind and then would walk until I came back into sight when he would then start to run again and that's how he beat me home. From the day he told me this information, he never beat me again.

Running was always my favourite thing as a child and it's still my favourite thing to do now. As soon as I could walk, I ran everywhere.

At school, academically, "just above average" but excelling in sport, sports days, inter-schools and inter-county running races when I just came alive. Some of my earliest memories are running with the boys at school and beating them in all the races. It gave me such a buzz.

My junior school teacher Mr King would sometimes take me for a cross country run at lunch time and once turning eleven, with his encouragement I joined the local athletics club. At a relatively young age this meant only training three times a week at the club but I would run on my own in between club nights.

Mum and Dad encouraged my brother Daniel and I to take part in any hobbies we were interested in. Dan was much more interested in more peaceful and relaxing hobbies and loved falconry, owning a couple of licensed kestrels and a buzzard which he would take out for country walks and sometimes fly at exhibitions.

We are like chalk and cheese, my brother and I. Dad built Dan his own aviary in the garden to keep his falcons in and Dan would weigh them daily before flying them. He told me once (well more than once I'm sure) that it was a pain having me as a sister as all the PE teachers at school would put him forward for everything – things he really didn't want to do, purely because he was my younger brother. I'm sure he could have made a good triathlete himself but he wasn't that way inclined and a much more chilled person. I did experience something similar myself one year. The school needed competitors for a squash tournament. Just because I could run, they put me forward for it (being short on numbers). It only ever happened the once.

My friends knew what to expect and came along to watch, laugh and mock me. (Or in their words "support me"). I was mortified to see them but they had good entertainment value for quite a while from that one. The ball went everywhere except where it was supposed to, or I missed it completely, one ball even ended up wedged behind a ceiling light, in the gallery where my "supporters" were stood.
Strangely I was never asked to play squash or any other racket sport ever again. I have zero hand, eye coordination, seriously – Zero!!

For some time, ballet and gymnastics were also my thing, attending clubs for both. Then there was skating, working through my figure skating awards and eventually joining the athletics club in addition to the other clubs. I would attend Church with my Dad Sunday morning, wearing my tracksuit because training was straight after. Never giving any thought to the time my parents gave up, taking me to these places let alone the cost. Neither Mum or Dad mentioned it or ever complained but I should imagine they were grateful as I became older and needed to prioritise my activities rather than trying to do everything.

Some sports complement each other but some work against each other and surprisingly ballet and gymnastics come under the later. My ballet teacher was not happy with me continuing with gymnastics as the two work the muscles in opposite directions. Gymnastics was first to go, followed by skating. Dad was disappointed when I finally gave up ballet to focus on my running …. "Anyone can just RUN" he said.

I soon joined a training group of girls at Solihull athletics club with a fantastic coach called Keith Wilson who must have had the patience of a saint to put up with bickering, teenage girls in his spare time. Vicky, (daughter of Keith) trained in that group and was a quality runner particularly over the 800-meter distance. We are still in touch, although she loves to travel with her work at international schools so we enjoy time together when she is visiting the UK. It always passes too quickly and when we met after my cancer, collecting her from the local train station, we just stood and hugged for the longest time. Neither wanting to let go. As always, it was wonderful to see her.

The group at the athletics club – (Solihull and Small Heath), raced cross-country in the winter and track in the summer. In the early days my parents would take me to all these races or occasionally as Dan was a few years younger, I would go with just my Dad so Dan wouldn't have to come – the track races would often mean heats and finals for multiple distances so a really long day. Cross-country was often wet and cold and whoever was with me would walk or jog the course before the race to check out danger spots. I have always been more than a little clumsy. One favourite comment to the rest of the girls was "just run behind Sam, she will find the holes and fall down them and then you can all avoid them all." Cross-country was not my favourite thing, mainly due to the resulting injuries.

My favourite distance on the track was always the 800 meter but the 1500 meter produced the best results for me and so that soon became the race I competed in most and soon became my favourite. Sometimes though I would be asked to race in the shorter distance relays which were always great fun but made me very nervous. Mostly running for myself, when put in a team situation, I would worry about letting the others down.

The highest level reached in my running was County Champion and then Midlands Champion. I can't recall which years these were but held multiple titles over various distances from 800m, 1500m and the 3000m. Looking back I wish I had raced more over 3000m and tried the 5000m but I so loved those shorter distances back then and wasn't really prepared to try anything else.

Admittedly as a young athlete I was a fairly bad loser and still now am criticised all the time for being too hard on myself. I'm also frequently told I lack confidence or self-belief. Eventually my parents understandably, went through a phase of not enjoying my attitude and racing. My lovely, thoughtful Mum one day bought me a gorgeous pair of gold earnings as a congratulations present for a race I was expected to win. It was a big event at Alexander Stadium and she brought them to the race in anticipation of the win. I finished second. Mum still wanted me to have her gift and offered them to me at the end. I crossly replied "I don't want them! I don't deserve them!"... and stormed off. What a horror!

Even through those "difficult years" when Mum and Dad were less keen on taking me racing, Keith, my coach was always there, without fail. He would drive to my house, collect me, take me to a race and drop me back off home at the end of the day, freely giving up his spare time. His wife Chris was always very supportive too. I can honestly say, there was never a race that I wanted to do but was unable to get to, someone always made it happen for me somehow. I was very lucky.

Gradually the other girls in the running group stopped racing and training but Keith still coached at the club mostly now coaching male athletes and myself. Around my mid-twenties, for a short time I trained with a good mixed group at Birchfield Harriers as it suited where I worked, in Birmingham. I soon missed Keith's enthusiasm and advice and bounced straight back to him. Feeling nervous about going back and that I had let him down, I cautiously approached him but he welcomed me back, no questions asked and from the first session it was like I had never left.

Lucky for me, I continued to train with Keith as my coach and an inspiring athlete called Steve Howes. By this age (old enough to know better) I was hopeless at knowing when to take easy days or easy weeks and didn't have any knowledge of massage and its huge benefits so just ploughed on running and running until injury occurred, took the enforced rest and went swimming until I could return to my beloved running. Even if Keith told me to take an easy day, it's doubtful I would have. I also enjoyed a very active social life which didn't help with performance.

Realising time was running out, age wise to really get the best results I was capable of with the events I loved, made me want to train even more relentlessly, but not at the cost of my social life. Not a great attitude and obviously created more injuries but I only realised that as an older athlete and after moving on.

The athlete I was doing most training with was Steve. He had moved from track racing to triathlon but was still strong on the track and cross-country and still a great runner.

I absolutely loved our training sessions and still miss them so much but as an older athlete I know what I can cope with before physically breaking down and sadly, these have been off the cards for a long, long time. Some of my favourites were –

1 mile reps on the track with one to one recovery. So, if it took 6 minutes to run the 1 mile you took the same time in recovery and went again or sometimes, we would go off heart rate – get it below 100 and off you go again – normally 6 of these.

400m reps on the track with 1 minute recovery – up to 16 of these.

200m reps on the track with 200m jog recovery x 4 – 4 sets of these

Hill reps in the winter up to 20 of these up a long muddy hill in Elmdon park. Always on a Sunday morning and normally feeling a little jaded to start after a Saturday night on the beer.

Mid-week, when not training the track, we ran a ten-mile route around Solihull and Knowle. During these runs I could see Steve looking out the corner of his eye, watching me and winding up the pace, just enough. If he thought he was dropping me he would ease very slightly and then start to crank it up again. I never let on I knew what he was up to but felt very lucky to have such a great training partner.

No weather conditions would put either of us off. It also didn't deter Keith who would stand track side with a stop watch, encouragement and advice, even in the freezing cold and pouring rain, when he had been at work all day. We trained in some shocking conditions but always enjoyed it. Well, I did, I can only assume Steve did too. As for Keith, he never ever complained about how long we were on the track, running well into the night with our endless repetitions.

Eventually after a number of problems, I became disheartened with the injures picked up as a runner, training sometimes twice a day. All that intensity and miles but I could never quite reach my England selection due to injuries at unfortunate times. This clearly wasn't helped by not having the best attitude in terms of socialising, late nights and drinking.

My personal best times were –

800m – 2:09

1500m – 4:28

3000m – 10:28

5000m – Although it doesn't count, on a treadmill, I ran 15:28 which if I had focused on would have been my strongest distance but I wouldn't sacrifice my 1500m to even give it a try. Again, poor attitude.

Steve suggested I give triathlon a go.

So, one early morning in September, Steve and I headed to Sheffield to take part in a standard distance triathlon. The standard distance is 1500m swim, 40km bike, 10km run. I would always advise someone to start with a sprint and a pool swim as their first triathlon but in my naivety and lack of knowledge and experience, didn't really give the distances much thought.

Unprepared for a triathlon, with no bike of my own at the time, I removed the shopping basket from my Mums Peugeot bike which she kindly lent to me to race with. This bike still had the gear changer on the down tube and most of the gears didn't work but at least it had two wheels and a chain that went round so no worries! Unlike my recent races where I worry about every minute detail, for this first ever attempt at triathlon, I knew nothing so didn't worry, and perhaps just assumed that everything would be fine - It's true sometimes ignorance is bliss.

Back then we didn't have to wear a wetsuit depending on water temperature but as it was September the water would have been warm enough for the 12-degree limit enforced now days anyway. Below that, wetsuits are mandatory now. At the time, not owning a wetsuit either, I dug out my speedo two-piece swim costume. Steve was quite shocked but in true fashion ditched his wetsuit in support and raced in his trunks.

Being so inexperienced that race was great, I enjoyed it all without any worries or pressure. It was interesting starting the run after the bike. Until you become practiced at this your legs feel most peculiar when you exit T2 to attempt running. Your legs do not feel real, like they are not attached to your body, its most odd and as my running was my strength, I hadn't practiced this part of the event. I soon settled into my running though, overcoming the jelly legs that all triathletes feel, although it did take a mile or so. It was great seeing Steve on the course too, shouting encouragement as we passed each other going the opposite direction.

After the finish, Steve, as always waited for the presentation and prizegiving as he normally wins his age group or is highly placed but to my utter amazement, they announced my name as first female.

The jelly legs must have returned as I stepped up to receive first prize, shocked that I had won. The prizes were great in those days too. Sadly, triathlon now is incredibly expensive to enter, with often very poor prizes or even none at all except a small trophy – the worst one I received for a first place has to be a pair of verruca socks and a swim hat. No joke! But for that first triathlon experience in Sheffield, it had been fairly cheap to enter and had great prizes. My first ever triathlon and I had won. I loved the event and of course I loved winning.

Racing with my good friend and training partner Steve Howes

With brother Daniel.

Mum and Dad with Charlie

CHAPTER 4. Transitions

As my first few triathlon races went well, gradually a transition took place where I raced less track and cross-country and more triathlons, racing over both sprint and standard distance.

The sprints are normally 750m swim (or 400m if in a pool) 20 or 25km bike and a 5k run and although short (for me), they are accessible distances for nearly everybody. At this time, they were hugely popular with big fields of all abilities, and so they always had a great atmosphere and were always good fun.

After racing a few standards and sprints and achieving good results, another friend – Sophie, who was racing triathlon for Great Britain encouraged me to try and qualify for team GB. Taking a big gulp and training more specifically, I followed her advice. I was over the moon when I made the qualification and raced a number of times in the GB team for both sprint, standard and also Duathlon, winning a bronze medal at the world championships in 2010. Duathlon is run 10k, bike 40k and run another 5k. In my opinion these are much harder on the legs but as the swim is my weakest discipline and such a worry for things to go wrong, I found Duathlon a very enjoyable experience for a while.

Around the time I started racing more triathlons and less track, I met Andy. We both trained at David Lloyd gym in Solihull. We would see each other in passing and just say hello. We had also bumped into each other a couple of times at races where we recognised each other from the gym. One evening a personal trainer at our gym introduced us properly and we got chatting, mostly about fitness, training and racing, it was great to chat to someone with the same passion and interests as myself.

We hadn't realised at the time but we were both going through a divorce, and soon to become single again. When the divorces came through, we made the most of it. We were both always out training, racing and partying pretty much constantly, separately at first, but this was to change.

Andy offered to take me open water swim training to a lake near Birmingham named Swan pool but referred to by Andy and his mates as "Swamp pool." It was pretty dirty, with algae and who knows what lurking below the surface, (though I have raced in far worse since). We would meet after work and head through Birmingham to this lake which was indeed, quite swampy. One evening we met after work as planned, but the wind was howling and bitterly cold and the rain torrential, everyone else had cried off, "Shall we go for some dinner instead?" suggested Andy. I didn't need much persuasion and really that was that.

...ether all the time after that dinner
...d each other through our divorces
...yed some fabulous nights out at the Jam
...ouse in Birmingham regularly dancing into the small hours.

The shorter distances were still going well for me, but it was obvious that longer events were calling, although not Ironman events at that time. Ironman had not really registered as anything I wanted to do, with me often saying "That's crazy, I'll never race Ironman distance" but Andy was ahead of me on his triathlon journey and later that year, was heading to Lanzarote to take part in one of the toughest Ironman events on the circuit and he asked me to go along for support. He already had a group of friends going with him but he persuaded me to go too. It was a great week, we never stopped laughing…….. Well apart from after the race when we missed each other and Andy spent a while shivering wondering where we all were and we stood near the finish wondering where he was. The reunion wasn't great but we made up for it the next day. I thought he was mad racing Ironman and was in awe really of what he had achieved. He was actually fine the next day too and recovered very quickly.

It was inspiring watching Ironman Lanzarote and Andy racing but obviously I would never contemplate racing a full Ironman…. however, he did persuade me to give a half Ironman a go so Andy and I trained together more and more for the half Ironman UK in 2001 held in North Wales.

At this point in my life, I was more determined to party than train, so my effort was limited and on race day I mostly enjoyed the scenery and really didn't take it seriously. Even setting up the bikes the day before the event, Andy was struggling putting both his bike and my bike together and getting the drinks ready while I lounged around and admired the location, not helping at all, and just being focused on irrelevant chatting.

"I love this scenery but where has the sun gone?" I muttered.

"Tell you what why don't you put some drink in your bottle?!" was Andy's reply...

I don't think he was too impressed but we laughed about it after and it's still a source of amusement now all these years later. As a Boswell you can never live something like that down. Everything is logged throughout the year to announce at the family Christmas get together.

So, Andy had inspired me to try a half Ironman. Half Ironman is obviously half the full distances, so 1900m swim, 90km bike, 21.1km (half marathon) run. As this was my first attempt at the distance and I was still equally focused on going out and partying, I was able to race with no pressure and thoroughly enjoyed the experience.

Being in North Wales, it was a very hilly course with some great scenery and I loved every second. Finishing third in my age category with a time not that far from some of the professionals, (despite my less than professional commitment.) Of course, I couldn't wait to do more and it quickly became my favourite distance and still is today. With half Ironman distance or 70.3 as it is now known (total distance in miles covered during the event) I found I could still very much have a good balance of everything else without too much extra time needed to train.

The following year I raced this event again and finished second in my category. If I'd bothered to go to the after-race presentation instead of dancing and celebrating at the local night club with friends, I would have found I had qualified to attend the World Ironman championships in Hawaii that year. But I had missed it! What a fool! However, I was now definitely a triathlete fool and no longer a pure runner.

There were so many times as a younger athlete and not so young, as with the early half Ironman days, that if I had been more dedicated, I could have achieved so much more. Obviously now in my

50's and having gone through major trauma and surgery with my cancer, I will never and believe have never reached my potential. I always put it down to bad luck but looking back it was clearly bad (or just the wrong) attitude. Athletes need it all to get to the very top – talent, help, support, luck and the right attitude, the latter being something I was very much lacking.

A few years after this transition from running to triathlon there was to be another transition - in my work life. Leaving school at 16, keen to start working and earning my own money, I went straight into work as a bank clerk at Barclays Bank. Then after a few years there moved into the accounts department at Britvic (part of Bass group), and then moved into IT support. Several years later I spent a short time at Sema group in IT support before moving in 1997 to Cap Gemini, an international IT and business consulting company, with local offices in Aston, Birmingham. I worked for various clients and was promoted into a more managerial role which I loved right from the start.

When I eventually became pregnant with Charlie, I worked up to two weeks before the due date before taking maternity leave. It came as a huge shock, while on leave that the entire department in Aston was to be moved to Inverness. Cheaper premises, cheaper work force. When it was time to return, HR advised me, my position was still available, based in Inverness or an alternative but similar role in London. Obviously reluctant to leave my baby to return to work anyway but to work in those locations just was not going to happen.

Eventually, after numerous phone calls and emails, a position became available on a client site in Birmingham, still working for Cap Gemini but based on a client site in the town centre. It was not managerial and was returning back to a support role. I gratefully accepted the position, just to earn money and return to work, but in IT, particularly technical roles everything changes over just a few months let alone the years I had not been technical for. Truth be known I was never very technical anyway and had much preferred the managerial and logistical type roles.

So, I had a new baby and was working in a role I was not comfortable with, which was also very inflexible. The positives were, my working week was only three days and the other members of the team were lovely people. It was a very flat structure though, so no room for change or promotion. I was stuck and didn't know what else to do. Eventually I became so unhappy there, I knew a change was needed.

Realising this sounds incredibly weird, one night I had a dream that I was a sports massage therapist, helping people overcome injuries and escape pain and I was really happy and content. I awoke saying to myself, "Ermmm where on earth did that come from?!" I spoke to Andy the next day and decided that's what I wanted to do. My entire life was around sport – why would I work in IT?!

I had been inspired by a Physio we knew so took the required courses for sports massage and retrained. At one stage I was working three days a week for a client of Cap Gemini, working evenings plus every Saturday and Sunday as a sports massage therapist, training for triathlon and raising a young child. It was a pretty crazy time but probably my biggest strength is time management, so I always found the time and motivation to spin these plates without letting any of them fall. Some nights though my working day wouldn't finish until 10pm and eventually Andy sat me down and said "What the hell are you doing? We never see you anymore and this isn't why you re-trained. You were never supposed to have the two jobs. You need to make a decision."

He was right of course, and what needed to be said but I still wrestled with that decision. Leaving safe employment was difficult to walk away from. I had been employed with sick pay, good pensions, paid holiday and guaranteed monthly income for around thirty years. I knew I could not continue with the routine I was in though, so eventually made the decision and left my IT role to become a full-time sports massage therapist.

Much like my dream, I immediately felt more content and thoroughly happy in my work. I love helping people to keep training and racing or just to stay active and be free from pain. I'm fortunate to work with some top athletes, older and younger and the older athletes (yes even older than me) give me inspiration. It's great to spend time with likeminded people and talk about shared interests and experiences, instead of being in an inflexible job that I didn't enjoy and being thought of as particularly odd for my out of work interests.

The satisfaction from helping to keep people racing or training or out of pain and discomfort is tenfold compared to fixing a laptop or patching in a network connection. I also enjoy helping with other, non-sporting injuries or niggles caused from anything such as long hours behind a wheel, hours sat at a desk and computer or walking around with a child on the hip – they are all things I can completely relate to.

Even years after making this work change, it's as enjoyable as much now as it was at the start. Most sporting niggles I have experienced myself and know the best way to overcome them and recover. I still love my job and just wish I had made the move a lot earlier.

First time racing for team GB. Front left

CHAPTER 5. Turbulent times.

2017 was a difficult year. My lovely Mum had become very poorly with a combination of Alzheimer's and vascular dementia and sadly passed away in the November of that year. We had been very close and I missed her so much, still do and always will. She was a great friend, would always be ready to listen and had a brilliant sense of humour, still making me laugh when she was so poorly.

It's such a cruel illness and had a huge effect on the family. My Dad was amazing and insisted on caring for Mum with very little help, right until a few months before her passing. Eventually on one of the GP visits, when they had to be called out, the GP had very stern words with both Dad and I about lifting Mum and what was best for us and more importantly Mum.

This finally convinced Dad what was required and Mum was moved to a nursing home where they did a superb job of looking after her. Dad may as well have moved in with her, he was there every waking hour and eventually the nursing home had to ask him to come in a bit later each day to allow them time to get Mum up and dressed. They were previously waking her from her sleep as Dad was there so early every day, desperate to be with her.

He totally worshiped Mum and her passing must have been so incredibly hard for him. It was hard for me too and with this condition, it's a strange and terribly sad feeling, but you miss the person and the times you shared even while they are still alive.

We were fortunate to have local friends whom I had always known as Aunty Kath and Uncle Orm. Actually, Ormand was Mums cousin so not really Aunty and Uncle at all but I had grown up seeing them at the very least every Christmas and summer.

During the period when Mum was poorly but still at home, they visited every Friday to allow me to continue working and Dad to do his shopping at a time that suited him. The arrangement I had put in place to help him, where I would sit with mum on a Saturday afternoon didn't fit with Dad's favourite time to shop. So I'm very grateful to "Aunty" Kath and "Uncle" Orm for helping in this way when things were so hard for us. Mum and Kath always had a real giggle together too, being friends from their teenage years.

There were a number of things that crept up with this illness. Some I was aware of and thought that's not right, and others I only realise looking back that the illness must have affected her behaviour far earlier than I realised. I would occasionally think Mum was being surprisingly mean to me or uncaring but throughout her life, her character had only been to care and support us, I now realise it must have been the illness changing her way of thinking, this was simply not my Mum at all.

It often takes a great deal of time to have this condition diagnosed and some days I would doubt myself as Mum would seem back to her old self. Confident, bright, caring and funny. I would think, I'm being silly she is fine, only for a few days later something to seem seriously wrong. I feel for anybody having a loved one going through this illness or who has lost someone to it and it must be so confusing and frightening actually having the condition and feeling that the world and the people in it are making less and less sense.

We tried, when we could to take some humour from some situations. There was one time that we laugh over now, though it was not at all funny at the time. Mum was still driving, as it was quite early on and we were a way off a diagnosis. She told Dad she was off to meet Kath at the local pub "The Hare and Hounds" and off she went… Leaving her bag behind. Dad noticed and thought she would need her bag with her purse in and as I was working, he better get it to her. As Mum had the car he hopped on his bike – which had a flat tyre, threw Mums handbag over his shoulder and cycled to the pub. It's only a couple of miles away but it's a main road and up a painfully long, steep hill. He must have looked a right sight, with a handbag over his shoulder and a flat tyre, struggling up that hill. He arrived exhausted to find Kath but no Mum. "Where is Jan?" Kath asked.

"I thought she was with you." replied Dad.

It took a while to think what could have happened and they must have been so worried. On this occasion I was oblivious and happily working away. Dad cycled home (still with the handbag and still with a flat tyre) in case Mum had come back for her bag. He waited a while there for her but still no sign of Mum.

Kath phoned for a progress report and said to Dad "I'm going to The Hopwood, that's the other place we sometimes go."

"OK." Said Dad and hopped back on his bike, handbag over the shoulder of course.... he arrived at the pub to find Mum patiently waiting in the car, staring into space. She must have been there for ages. It was a clear sign something wasn't right.

I still raced that year; it helped keep me positive, but competed over the sprint distances. Sometimes Dad would need me to help out, and I wanted to be local with some reserves of energy, not three hours away from home on a bike. There were times I would be in a spin class at the gym or going out for the day with Charlie and I would get a call from Dad with another problem he would need help with.

My "A" race that year was the World Championships in Rotterdam. I finished 6th on a technical course. It's definitely not my best distance and a technical bike and unrehearsed transitions left me lacking there but I did manage the same run time as the winner Michelle Jones, (previous Olympic Gold medallist) so I took some comfort from that.

As we were keeping the trip short, not wanting to be away too long, I treated us to stay at the British team hotel. It was so good to be around the rest of the team and the hotel was gorgeous, probably the most luxurious hotel we have ever stayed in. Complete with roof top pool and sauna, with slippers and robes in the room and a bath tub large enough to swim in. Rotterdam is also a beautiful city. I'm a country girl, but can recommend Rotterdam to anyone as a city break, lots of open space and waterways, a great cycle lane infrastructure and some quirky cafes with excellent coffee and cakes.

We have been to some fabulous places through my racing, places we would never normally have even thought of visiting and Charlie, who has always loved the events, particularly the internationals, is very well travelled for his age.

By 2018, after Mum's passing the previous year, I was itching to race long again so returned to Ironman racing in Vichy, France. It was a fairly easy location to get to and as usual we planned to have a family holiday after the race, moving onto Il de Oleron on the Atlantic coast, so Charlie could partake in his much-loved surfing.

The race has some great memories for me, particularly as I had the chance to race with Steve again, the very person who had tempted me to give triathlon a go all those years back. Steve travelled with his lovely wife and daughter, we all had a lot of giggles and apart from the great company, I found it really helped with my normal pre-race nerves!

The race itself was tough. It was a surprisingly cold and foggy start, but I had a good swim (1hr8) and strong bike. Despite being totally unprepared (kit wise) for the cold start, completing the rolling bike route in 5hrs28. Unfortunately, as usual the run wasn't great. We knew at this stage, at the age of 47, I was training and racing with quite severe anaemia due to "women's problems". I had large fibroids and my GP had instructed me to have surgery later that year.

I believe being anaemic greatly affected my performance in this race. The sun came out and the heat built as my energy dwindled. I had a disappointing "run" (though most of it was walked) in 4hrs17 placing me 5th in my category at the finish. No Hawaii qualification with that performance.

Steve and I shared a laugh the next day though, discussing our various performances and the fact that his bike had rattled some parts free on the terrible road surface on sections of the course. We also had a lovely family holiday after the race so I couldn't be too upset.

After the Vichy Ironman in 2018 it became apparent, I needed a hysterectomy and sooner rather than later. I was permanently anaemic and even the strongest iron tablets were not helping.

Another trip to the GP to hear her say "I simply cannot allow this to continue. You need surgery and as soon as possible."

"Can I go private and have it now – it's off season." Was my reply. We were very fortunate, Andy worked at Jaguar Land Rover (or JLR) at the time and had some fantastic private health care for all the family. Although actually I don't think he ever used it himself, I certainly did though.

I had the surgery, took 6 weeks out and started the slow road to recovery. By late spring of 2019 I was back racing and raced half Ironman in early summer. I then enjoyed some good winter training and looked forward to the 2020 race season where surely nothing could go wrong?

Ha!...

A world pandemic was coming.

Langdales, Lake district with Mum and Dad, early in Mums illness.

After Ironman Vichy 2018

CHAPTER 6. Covid, long Covid and Ironman UK.

Hello Covid!

Being one of the first in the UK to catch this awful virus, it hit me hard. I really was incredibly poorly, and of course we now know why. After two weeks of deteriorating health, slow at first and then following a rapid decline, was admitted to hospital. I was kept in for a couple of days before being allowed to return home. I didn't do things by halves, and the doctor took one look at the chest x-rays and diagnosed me as having "Covid with double pneumonia."

Four courses of antibiotics and steroids later with some broken ribs from excessive coughing and I was still no better. Starting with the virus mid-February, by June I could just about walk a mile. It made my hysterectomy recovery seem easy. Long covid then became an issue with aches and pains, sore throats, coughing and exhaustion all being long term constant companions. The pain around my kidneys in particular was excruciating. One day I would think I was recovering, Andy would say "You know, I think you are a little better today, you have coughed less and seem less tired."

The next day I would be worse than ever. It was very strange and extremely frightening - as it was for so many.

It was perhaps a sign there was more going on than Covid as the pain remained all around my kidneys. I couldn't understand why more people with Covid were not discussing this particular long-term symptom and the immense pain it caused. Eventually, months down the line, in late summer 2020, some 7 months after contracting Covid, I returned to a tiny amount of (slow) training. Building back some semblance of strength, whilst all the time managing my symptoms, just doing what I could when I could and resting more than I would have liked.

Even by 2021, I couldn't run with any sort of consistency; inflammation was a constant issue. Eventually, just to get myself back racing, I competed in an aquabike (swim, bike) and in the autumn a sprint duathlon but my running didn't really become consistent until the start of 2022… So then, for motivation, I entered Ironman UK 2022.

My long covid symptoms at last started to ease and my fitness stats started to show there was some improvement, with a 76 VO2Max reading for both bike and run. Happily, my resting heart rate was back to 31 beats per minute, sometimes at night dropping to 27. This didn't mean there was a problem. I have always had a very low resting heart rate and being that low was a sign my fitness was back after such a long slog recovering from Covid.

I started to feel fitter and did more and more training, having a great few months of tough cycle rides with my new cycling buddy Phil who was a huge help.

Again, I had some good fortune here, and couldn't believe my luck. No fan of riding on my own and in need of a new bike pal, Phil had just taken early retirement and also preferred to ride with company. He rides long – really, really long distances – 400kms and the like. He has ridden both the London Edinburgh London (or LEL, 1,500kms) and Paris Brest Paris (PBP – 1,200kms), long distance audaxes as well as other epic events with friends in the Beacon RCC. Clearly mad as cheese and also great company. Not only did we get on but we were perfectly paced for each other. Some days Phil was stronger and on occasion I was a little ahead but we always waited and encouraged each other and found things to talk about to take our mind off the pain, tiredness, rain and/or cold.

The ultra long 300-400kms rides were too long for me so I didn't ride those with Phil or any of the club but we established a great routine between us, riding 150 to 200km rides on a regular basis and then shorter faster rides with the others in the Beacon cycling club. I really grew to love cycling during this time, with the help and company of Phil and the rest of the group.

The group rides could become really frantic and were regularly well over 20mph. Head down, lined out, flying along, passing other groups out riding. I would have a huge grin on my face and couldn't help the occasional giggle to myself, it was so perfect and such an amazing buzz to be back out riding strongly and with a new set of friends to motivate and help me.

Even as 2021 wore on and my cycling form was coming back strongly, I was still struggling with the running and lack of consistency. Inflammation was still a constant issue whenever I tried to run a little quicker or a little longer. It was slow and painful. It really wasn't until early 2022, some two years later that I felt I could run with some consistency and relatively pain free… And I had Ironman UK to prepare for.

The preparation for Ironman UK 2022 eventually went well, considering I had been so poorly with long covid over the last two years. I had a longer than normal taper to allow my aging body to recover and felt well prepared for the race in early July. As part of the preparation, I also made contact with the Bolton triathlon club, as they were known as having friendly members and were always keen to help anyone signed up for this race. The club arranged practice days on the bike and run course which I took full advantage of, visiting Bolton a couple of times to recce the course with the local guys and girls. They were so generous with their knowledge, all telling me the sections to look out for, where the biggest potholes were, and where it may be possible to make up time.

One trip, only a few weeks before race day, we all completed two laps of the four-lap bike course followed by a lap of the four-lap run. The routes had changed considerably since 2016, when I last competed there so I wanted to experience the new course. The swim route remained the same so I didn't worry about that, swimming enough open water at home. The Bolton lake could wait until race day.

Finishing the run loop, I commented to the Bolton runner I was running with "Errm, I'm just going to carry on into the park. My Garmin is at 4.8 miles, I can't have that, it has to be 5".

"Me too" he said.

Next came Chris, another Bolton Tri member… "I'm just going to run into the park, I want to finish on five miles."

Shortly followed by Gale "I'll be back in a minute; I'm just going on to the park."

We all burst out laughing, every one of us sharing the same mentality.

Race day soon came round. The swim was a lake swim and although the heavens opened on the start line, it went well and I exited the water in first place in my category and highly placed overall. I always worry during the swim, mostly about collisions and having my goggles kicked off. Thankfully that didn't happen. I always swim wide, meaning I swim extra distance but safely. I advise any nervous swimmers to do the same. Transition 1 went smoothly and I was pleased to jump onto the bike in a strong position.

The UK Ironman is famous for being very hilly with almost 8000ft of climbing through mixed areas and at times some very rough, potholed roads. To be honest I totally loved this course apart from some of the descents … I've always been a big coward on the descents and my bike buddies often call me a "Sunday driver" or ask "where are your driving gloves, old lady?" Fair comments.

On this particular day, the weather was tough at times with some exposed sections and lots of rain on the higher parts of the course. I have never seen people just stop pedalling and pull over on the bike course but this was exactly what was happening on some of the longer climbs as the elements closed in.

The bike section seemed to finish surprisingly soon and I loved the route, despite the conditions, probably coping with the tough course better than most. I arrived back into transition 2 as first in my age group with now a lead of over 40 minutes to second in my age but also to shouts of "second lady overall". I heard this several times and riding into transition, I was surprised to find cameras filming me and only one other women's bike in transition. The cameras were just for local news but this was a new experience for me. It was a real shock and adrenaline rush...But then I started to worry - although my run has always been my strength in all other distances, I've yet to have a strong run at an Ironman. (sprint, standard, half Ironman – all great, full Ironman - not so much).

As I started the run as first in my age and second overall, with a significant lead, I felt comfortable…. Until I hit the first short sharp hill. I felt a sudden stab of pain in the right side of my abdomen and into the right hip flexor, something not experienced at all during training. Really worrying with a marathon ahead of me.

The run course is lumpy through the park and then approximately 2.5 miles up hill and 2.5 miles down, four times but a gradual hill, nothing steep and as I started to climb the gentle slog, the pain eased. Sadly, this was temporary and each steep climb through the park I was really in trouble and eventually couldn't recover. Soon having to resort to walking most of the marathon, in significant pain and losing all forty minutes of my lead to finish second in my age category.

I managed to make it into the top ten women overall and second in my age but after sitting second overall with such a strong lead, dropping those positions was deeply frustrating. Although pleased with the progress made since my experience with Covid, I was still disappointed with the thought of what could have been and the loss of my Hawaii qualification. Given what happened a few weeks later, it was for the best that I didn't win, but at the time, I was quite despondent.

Shortly after the race, I was very sick, unable to even keep water down, another sign something wasn't right. I have experienced this after full Ironman in the past but we believe (as did the surgery team) that the cancer had been there for a long time so it's likely I have raced with it there before. Poor Charlie had to sit with me whilst Andy went back to transition to try and collect my bike and kit, explaining the situation to the officials.

Charlie was concerned that he should be calling for an ambulance as I couldn't walk either. I had a plastic bag as a sick bag and some wonderful staff at the David Lloyd in Bolton also looking after me, even fetching me a wheel chair to enable me to make my way out to the car. Luckily Andy persuaded the marshals at transition and he was allowed to bring back my bike and kit before taking us all back to the hotel.

Strangely, I recovered remarkably quickly from the race. In fact, at 2am the following morning I was feeling well and made tea and ate chocolate muffins and bananas… Quietly so as not to wake Andy and Charlie. Not even feeling tired the next day, I knew I had to make myself rest but could have completed some light training by the middle of the week. I was excited about the thought of winter training, more races and going again next season.

We travelled home for some (reluctant) but well needed rest.

In the week that followed Ironman UK, at home relaxing, a few pounds lighter after the race and sickness, a large mass was very apparent in my right abdominal area. I was concerned but not overly so, assuming it was some irritation from the race and expected it to settle down over the next couple of days. I did start to become more concerned when there was no change over the following weekend. By Monday I was really worried, I still didn't think it was anything too serious but certainly wanted it checked, so booked in to see my GP. Immediately concerned he commented "I really don't like that" and put me on a rapid two-week assessment for scans and other unpleasant tests, sending me on my way with numerous Macmillan leaflets.

During that two week wait I consoled myself with the fact that it couldn't possibly be cancer, surely you can't race an Ironman with cancer. Turns out you can...

After an agonising wait for news, the specialist called me in, sat me down and told me I had a tumour in my abdomen and it was a sarcoma cancer. The tumour was 19cms across, approximately 5kg in weight and was growing in my abdominal cavity on the right, (where I had felt the pain during the race). Andy and I sat in the consulting room in disbelief and horror. It was just such a shock and even after receiving this news, I knew the worst thing was that we had to come home to tell our beautiful boy.

No tears were shed and it didn't even seem real, until I had to break the news to Charlie. I just kept repeatedly saying how sorry I was and couldn't stop crying at the thought of putting him through this. He sat with a protective arm around me for the entire evening, telling me with utter conviction that I was going to be OK and everything was going to be fine.

He totally amazed me and was a power of strength throughout the entire experience. I was then, and always will be so incredibly proud of him.

The hard work in getting over this, the uncertainty over whether I would live and the pain I felt that I possibly wouldn't see Charlie grow as an adult started that day. The next few months were a time I will never, ever forget for many, many reasons.

Let's come back to this at the end….

End of Stratford half marathon 2022 – training for IMUK

Winning age group at Outlaw 2022 – half Ironman in prep for IMUK

IMUK 2022 Finish

CHAPTER 7. Training and race tips

Through my work and because of my race experience, I am often asked for help and advice about training and competing in triathlons. So, I thought it may be useful to share some of the tips that I have followed or learnt the hard way. Although an old(ish!) working Mum, I do have bags of amateur experience so you may find some of the tips in this chapter helpful, I hope so.

Disclaimer here first though, when it comes to triathlon training, most coaches would look at my training history and say that it has not been specific or targeted enough, it's too basic and I could improve if I trained "properly". The trouble is, if I see a complex training plan full of tiny segments of high-end efforts, heart rate changes, swapping swim strokes every couple of lengths and/or breaking training down into complicated mixed sessions I just switch off. That's just the way I am, others may be motivated by this.

I have always preferred to keep training simple, but having said that would always recommend that any training and racing you do, you keep a record. That way you can look back on what worked well and what did not. You can normally look back on your training if you have a niggle and pinpoint errors that may have caused, or at the very least contributed towards the problem and adjust your future training accordingly.

My normal training schedule is six sessions a week, and you won't be surprised to learn that this is broken down into two swims, two bike rides and two runs. These are shorter and faster if racing sprint to middle distances that year or longer and less fast (which sounds better than slow) if I am training specifically for an Ironman. That is honestly as technical as it gets. This is mostly down to being self-coached as a triathlete and working out what suits me. I would say that is the most important thing, we are all different and what works for me, might not be the best for you. Learn from your experiences. My methods suit me because I want to stay consistent across all three disciplines. I could risk changing my training to try and improve but my methods work for me and unless I do something foolish (or become poorly) they seem to work well. Racing for over forty years, at least twenty of those as a self-coached triathlete, I find the consistency is what brings results, so I'm very reluctant to change.

The importance of a good, regular sports massage should not be underestimated. This isn't just because it's what I do for work, it's what works. Massage helps to ease out niggles and tight muscles, generate extra blood flow and allows me to train hard when I need to.

I was lucky enough to be introduced to a fantastic physio when I was struggling with a calf injury, training for my first GB race all those years ago. Neil had vast amounts of experience, working with top premier league footballers and many other athletes, he only ever used different methods of massage on me - and I went with a lot of niggles! I then found if I had regular sports massage as a preventative measure, most niggles were kept at bay or resolved quickly. Neil had previously treated Andy and was kind enough to show us some great techniques which we could apply ourselves.

In my opinion, it isn't possible to train hard and not have muscle tensions or knots of some kind. It just makes sense to treat them regularly as a matter of routine rather than attempt to train through them, particularly as an older athlete. I was actually astounded by what massage could accomplish, and this is what led me to completely change my career path, from IT to sports massage.

So, here's my short list of good practice, which will help you keep training and therefore, improving.

Sports Massage

A good and effective sports massage needs to be firm but not too aggressive. The muscles should be warmed up first before the massage goes deeper into the muscles to remove the knots or tensions and then flushed through after. This routine changes, depending on whether it is being used for injury prevention and maintenance or working on a specific niggle or injury. Make sure you take warm layers for after the massage and hydrate well. I am very lucky in that my husband regularly massages my legs and back for me, under my specific instructions of course (which as you can imagine sometimes doesn't go down well!) But I appreciate his efforts, and he has now become very effective at helping to minimise any muscular issues.

During race season we schedule in a massage almost every week. If this is not possible for you then during race season try every other week or at least once a month and then off season they can become a little less frequent, depending on your training. You can probably manage with less if you are in your 20's or 30's but like everything else, it becomes more and more important with age and your muscles need more maintenance. Though it also depends of course on intensity and frequency of training and racing.

Foam Roller

What is also fundamental to me and my own injury prevention is my regular use of a foam roller. If I did not have time to foam roll before a run – then I would not run. Purchase a good firm roller and use it regularly, don't just stick it in a corner to gather dust.

Other self-help tools

If I notice a tight area, I have various self-help torture tools to help in between massages and tell all my clients to use the same. A golf ball is useful for the plantar fascia area (arch of the foot). A lacrosse ball works deep into knotted areas of muscle, if the roller is not specific enough. I much prefer a lacrosse ball over a spiky ball as they seem to work deeper into the muscles. These are also good for tight trapezius muscles, which I often suffer with after work. As with the roller always make sure you are only working into soft tissue – not over bone or joints.

Injury

If the worst happens and a niggle occurs and does not settle within a few days, I find that if I take four weeks off running, have frequent massage, the problem is often resolved. Personally, most of my niggles are aggravated by running even if caused by something else, but I am usually able to continue swimming and cycling. It's often quicker to take the four weeks hit immediately. Certainly, do not fall into the habit of resting, testing, resting, testing – before you know it, you are six weeks down the line and you will have to take four consecutive weeks off anyway. Obviously, this would be different with more serious injuries and then advice from you GP or a physiotherapist is needed.

When returning from injury, do not push the pace and ensure you adhere to the ten percent rule. Do not increase distance, frequency or speed more than ten percent. Building back too quickly may result in further injuries or a return of the previous one.

Injury can also be caused from the bike, (apart from the obvious) specifically the bike setup or frame size. Many cyclists and triathletes prefer to book in for a "bikefit" but often a bike shop can be helpful, or there are some good books on bike setup.

Hydration and fuel

Pay attention to hydration and electrolytes. Dehydration can actually cause injuries. The body will take fluid from muscles to keep vital organs from being dehydrated, so the muscles themselves become even more dehydrated; this has the potential to cause cramping or muscle tears.

I have always used an energy drink with electrolytes on long sessions and just an electrolyte drink on short, sweaty sessions such as a fast bike, turbo or fast run. If you are someone who suffers with cramp or frequent minor tears, the solution may be as simple as increasing your hydration and electrolytes. During high exertion, particularly in hot weather or indoor sessions, the body sweats out sodium, zinc, potassium, magnesium and other nutrients vital to wellbeing. These nutrients are all needed for normal muscle and nerve function so need replacing. Hydrate well after sessions too, not just before and during.

Limit alcohol

Many will not like this tip; indeed, I did not follow it myself in my younger days, but now as an older athlete, during race season I never drink alcohol. If that is one compromise too far then just try to keep it very minimal and certainly do not indulge before major training sessions or racing. Alcohol reduces the body's hydration substantially and can contribute to inflammation; it is something else you can get away with as a youth but not as an older athlete.

Food and race nutrition

Try to take on plenty of protein, particularly straight after a hard session. In the past I have used a protein shake after intense or long sessions just to start refuelling as soon as possible and before showering. More recently, I prefer to use proper protein-rich food whenever possible. We eat a lot of eggs, chicken, fish and yoghurt and have normalised their use in our everyday family meals. This now, however (as with electrolytes) I have to take care and ensure I do not overdo the protein as it can be hard on my one remaining kidney. Hopefully this doesn't apply to you, but for me now protein shakes are certainly off the menu.

If you are racing and particularly if your event is long such as an Ironman or even a 70.3 half Ironman, check the race website for details on where the feed stations are and more importantly what food or energy bars/gels will be present at the stations. Train with whatever they are using to make sure you can tolerate it. I try to be as self-sufficient as possible on race day though and carry what is needed. Everything carried, I have tested and know suits me and won't result in stomach cramps.

Rest

I'm definitely not very good at this one but it does help hugely if you can give yourself sufficient rest days or longer rest periods, it's when the body recovers. I always aim to have one day off from any training each week but should probably be off my legs more than I am, often choosing to work more or catch up with friends or tend to housework or the garden. I know pro cyclists on their days off, largely stay on the sofa and rest their legs, but they are pro cyclists after all, in effect paid to sit around on their days off, most of us have to get on with our lives.

Kit

For sprint distances I always use an all-in-one tri suit and for half and full Ironman a two piece. The one piece has less seams for a pool swim and I need all the help I can get for that. The two piece allows for easier toilet breaks on the longer races and is normally worn under a wetsuit for the open water swim.

Use elastic laces in your run shoes. My transitions are not great but these obviously save time. Keep them just for racing though, as they do not seem to offer the same support in the shoe as using proper laces. One year I trained some substantial miles in the same shoes I was racing in and kept the elastic laces in. I'm sure this contributed to a niggle that year. I haven't made that mistake since.

In the same way as testing your race food and drinks, then always make sure you train with and test any kit you intend to race in, including your trainers, running vests and tri suits. Don't leave anything to chance on the day. There is enough that can go wrong without some sort of unexpected chafing to deal with. Also (although this sounds obvious) set out your kit the day before, or even better put everything in your car ready to go and count it off your mental checklist. I know of fellow athletes who have arrived at a race with no cycling helmet packed, and couldn't race. Another, a friend of mine turned up to a sprint triathlon with two left trainers and no right trainer after he hurriedly threw them into the car, in the dark, on the morning of the race. He did race and thankfully it was a sprint but it still couldn't have helped. I confess, to also racing once with no cycle shoes, having left them at home. An on-site mechanic fitted pedals with straps to allow me to race but it obviously wasn't ideal.

Whilst on the subject of the race and events going wrong, when racing open water, as mentioned earlier, I always prefer to swim wide of the masses. I enjoy swimming but I do not enjoy getting clobbered by other swimmers and have learned through experience to swim in clear water even if it means swimming a little further. If you are confident in these situations though and a strong swimmer you will get some benefit from swimming in a pack or on another swimmer's toes, it's just not for me.

Race day kit and transitions

I have a check list to avoid the missing helmet/ two left trainer issue. You will want to make your own but you could use this as a start. For Ironman races, they use colour coded bags for each transition so my check list breaks it down into these swim, bike, run bags so may be a little over kill for shorter distances. I even include what to wear when I get up in the morning. Suffering terribly with nerves, my head is often not focused and having my list definitely gives me one less thing to worry about…..

Wear – tri suit, calf guards, warm layers, old trainers – non racing trainers as the shoes for racing will be put in transition. Take water proofs, cap, swim hat, goggles, spare goggles, electrolyte or energy drink, cereal bar, bike fuel to put on bike, toilet roll, warm clothes for after.

Bike bag – bike shoes, socks, helmet, race belt (attach number when you have it), sun glasses, gloves, spare contact lenses, extra gels or food which are not already on the bike. The spare contact lenses are an addition after I completed a half Ironman with one lens, after the other was washed away by heavy rain and floated off down the lake. I felt rather sick afterwards.

Run bag – gels, trainers, fresh socks, (more) spare lenses, drink system for long races plus salt tablets if needed. I recommend these for long races but be cautious and do some research. I doubt I could use them now but have used them in Ironman races before, particularly in warm conditions.

Ironman racing means racking your bike and above bags the day before the race. A good idea is to photograph everything you put into your bags. Then when you are lay awake all night worrying about your race and if everything has been put into transition, you can check the picture (and re check if you are like me). It's one less thing to worry about.

The night before the race and actually for a few days before, try to eat plain, non-spicey food. Also hydrate plenty – but don't overdo it. I gave myself hyponatremia at IMUK 2016 and had to check myself out of hospital the next day to go and collect my Kona slot. I had simply taken on too much water and not enough electrolytes during the race. I was lucky but it can be dangerous. Obviously, all this is less of an issue for shorter races, it's all about balance and learning from experience.

One final note for racing – always thank officials, marshals and supporters. Remember it's a privilege and a blessing to be able to compete, whether it is for a Kona slot, to improve on an age-group position or just finish so…. Smile!

CHAPTER 8. The Big C

Leaving this chapter until towards the end is largely due to how hard I found the entire experience, of having cancer and the huge surgery required, leading to such a long stay in hospital.

I would like to start the chapter by saying though how fortunate I am to have some wonderful friends and family who all helped a huge amount, right from diagnosis through the recovery process which is still ongoing. I also know some incredible people who work at the Queen Elizabeth hospital. I have not known them for a long period of time but they could not have helped me more and I feel blessed to have them and my family and friends in my life.

The surgeon who completed the operation is one of the most amazing people on the planet, I know I would say that wouldn't I. But it's true. The procedure required to remove the sarcoma which started deep in my abdominal cavity, is apparently the biggest surgery completed at the Queen Elizabeth (QE) hospital.

The sarcoma surgery team at the QE consisted of Fabio, Valentina, Mr Max Almond and Mr Sam Ford. They are all incredible human beings and I will never be able to thank them enough for what they did for me. During my stay I saw them all but mostly my actual surgeon, Fabio (I hope it's OK to use his first name, he checked in on me pretty much daily so it seems appropriate).

Fabio met with Andy and I some weeks before the operation, to tell us exactly what was going to happen. He outlined very clearly what a big and risky operation this was, despite their experience in dealing with these types of sarcomas. He also added that in almost all cases, a blood transfusion is required, due to the amount of blood lost during the surgery.

Fabio completed the surgery on Monday 26th September 2022, removing the huge cancerous tumour, but also had to remove one of my kidneys, an adrenal gland, part of my bowel, part of my abdominal wall, the fascia of the Psoas muscle and part of a tube leading to the heart. As mentioned, this was a big operation. Somehow this amazing man removed all of that in one mass, stitching up the internals as he went. Incredibly and highly unusually, such was his skill, a blood transfusion was not required. Fabio told me afterwards that my tumour weighed at least 5kgs.

The scar, from breast bone to pubic bone is 16 inches (41cm) but has healed nicely and is fading all the time. It is certainly a very small price to pay for the removal of "that thing!"

26th September 2022 will be permanently etched on my mind. I will never forget the date. I said goodbye to Charlie who gave me the longest hug saying "It's going to be alright Mum; I know it's going to be OK". I was shaking even then at the thought of not being there for him and the possibility of never being there for him again.

Andy and I travelled to the hospital almost in silence, both lost in our own thoughts and fears. Shortly after arriving, he had to leave me and return home as I was quickly moved into the pre-op area. Immediately, we started texting. Andy later told me he couldn't do or think of anything and the day lasted forever as he waited for news. He had left me just after 7:30am and Fabio called him when I was in recovery around 6:30pm. What an incredibly long day for us all! Fabio must have been totally exhausted… but then maybe this is a typical day for this talented surgeon.

Thankfully Andy was allowed to see me the very next day. I was in a fairly new unit called EPOC or (Enhanced Post Operative Care). This unit provided ITU like care for patients undertaking complex surgical procedures. Andy said I looked like a cyborg, I had so many tubes feeding in or from my body. The tubes were feeding oxygen, an epidural plus another pain relief tube into my spine, two drains clearing the fluid from my abdominal cavity and two different IV lines for medication and tests.

Then there was a catheter as obviously leaving the bed as this stage was totally out of the question. It was quite a collection.

Looking after me in EPOC was a young female nurse who was incredibly thorough and caring. My friend Damian, a top anaesthetist at the QE was also around for a lot of the time and both gave me comfort in their knowledge and care. It felt so safe there and I felt so cared for that I really didn't want to leave EPOC after the two days when it was time for me to head to a general ward.

Being a terrible worrier at the best of times, you can imagine all my concerns and questions during this period… even worrying over the support team computer not being plugged in…In my defence, I was on a lot of strong pain relief and my brain was pretty scrambled!

Moving from the 24hour care of EPOC to a general ward was a big change. The ward sister was on long term sick and in addition all the staff were incredibly stretched. Some days there was a long delay in receiving my pain relief and medication. The pain was indescribable and like nothing experienced before and I hope never have to experience again. These were some of my lowest moments.

Amongst all the worry and pain and incredible work load on all the staff, there were some amazing nurses – Dan, Sharin, Nitish and Aneeta were all wonderfully caring nurses who somehow managed to always deliver medication on time and with a smile. They must have returned home after their twelve hour shifts totally exhausted. I would see one of these nurses arrive on shift and breath a huge sigh of relief, knowing the care would be excellent for the next three days or nights. As mentioned, Fabio visited almost daily and he or one of the team were always available should I have any concerns or questions. These daily visits made a huge difference to both me and also Andy who was at times very stressed.

Being a terribly light sleeper at the best of times, is another unfortunate trait of mine. With all the machines beeping, doors banging, drugs being administered, moaning and shouting patients and nurses doing their work, I didn't have much sleep at all during my two months stay. I would just be about to drop off and then would hear…."Sam, it's time to take your blood pressure"

A couple of hours later, "Sam, it's time to take your bloods."

An hour later lights on and "breakfast time!"

I was so incredibly low, but (particularly after witnessing some very rude behaviour towards one of the young nurses) I always, always replied with a friendly "It's no problem."

Sleeping tablets were available but stubbornly, every drug I managed without, I saw (rightly or wrongly) as a step towards recovery. I would have a minor celebration each time we managed to remove one of the many tubes or stop taking one of the many IV meds or tablets.

It seemed to be an eternity, this period in hospital. So many other patients would come and go and still I would be there. After two weeks of just lying there doing nothing, just as I thought I should surely be heading home soon, my temperature began to rise.

It became clear there was an infection somewhere but it was not obvious why or where it was located. Another CT scan was ordered and it was soon discovered I had a "collection", a pool of infection around the bowel part of the surgery. A drain had to be fitted. This is quite a traumatic experience too. A surgery team arrive at your bed and lots of local anaesthetic is injected, then a length of tube is inserted. This tube went through an incision into my back and down into my abdominal cavity where the infection was located. It requires skill and care when inserted so as not to damage any internal organs.

So, another tube went back in and additional antibiotics given via IV. With more tubes and more medication going back in, it was an obvious backward step for sure. I was so disappointed especially as it meant another two weeks in hospital, away from my beautiful boy and another two weeks without sleep in my clanging, banging, beeping ward.

After that depressing extra couple of weeks, around the end of October (over a month after the surgery) the sarcoma team thought the infection had cleared and I was well enough to return home at long last.

It was a memorable journey home. Leaving those medical experts at the hospital with all the pain relief and lifesaving drugs. After over a month in hospital with advice and help nearly always at hand, I had to really focus on my breathing for the entire journey. I was so frightened and what should have been a joyous journey home was actually terrifying. Maybe a part of me suspected that this next stage in my recovery would be short lived. Nevertheless, once home my Garmin watch went on and Andy and I walked for a quarter of a mile outside in the fresh air.

The next morning, I luxuriated in my own shower and dressed in some different clothes. Over the next day or two, it was lovely to see some friends and family for just short visits but sure enough, within less than a week, I began to feel poorly again. I thought perhaps I had just been doing too much so backed off the walking and stopped the visitors from coming round. I was still deteriorating though and after a couple of days I could not eat or even drink anything without feeling incredibly nauseous. Eventually I couldn't even sip water and admitted to Andy, "Something is really wrong. We need to go back to hospital."

Charlie gave me one of his medicinal hugs, telling me "Don't worry Mum, it won't be as bad this time, you will be home before you know it."

Back we went to the QE. Andy was not allowed to stay. I spent a full day, sitting alone in an assessment ward waiting to see Fabio who was probably busy saving more people in the operating theatre.

Eventually Fabio arrived and after a short inspection and a check over the bloods which had been taken earlier, he readmitted me. Back to the same ward I had so recently escaped, with what was quickly diagnosed as another infection. By the time I was wheeled back on the ward, my body was expelling everything through severe sickness and diarrhoea. (Sorry if that's too much information).

The next day Fabio came to see me and yet another CT scan was ordered. The results showed what the doctors and I had both expected, it was another "collection". This time it was clear the bowel part of the surgery had not repaired and everything that should have been leaving my body through that route as waste was free roaming around my body and blood stream.

I had E-coli, some other nasty bacterial infection and sepsis was even mentioned, so it was no wonder everything had gone haywire internally. Another drain was quickly inserted, another IV line put in and more antibiotics were fed through the line. I was mortified with this setback and knew it was going to be another long stint of recovery in that noisy ward. There was another addition to this stay. In order to allow the bowel to repair I had to be put on nil-by-mouth for a much longer time.

I had only spent a few days nil-by-mouth after the surgery and this was soon changed to being allowed a reduced diet. This time, being nil-by-mouth would be for much, much longer.

Obviously, we all need fuel, so to keep me alive during this period, I had to receive fluids through another IV line plus calories through a PICC line (peripherally inserted central catheter).

A PICC line is fed into the large central veins near the heart and puts calories into the body, thereby avoiding the stomach and digestive system, allowing that part to rest and hopefully repair. So yes, lots more tubes back in, lots more medication and what was to be another month in hospital.

During this time another friend, Claire – wife of Damian and anaesthetist in cardiology at the same hospital, would pop in to see me. Sometimes I was so exhausted I could barely speak, but after a long shift, she would still sit by me when she could and offer comfort and advice, before returning home to her three children. Such a kind and generous act of friendship which meant so much and gave me an immense amount of reassurance.

Due to the lasting effects of the Covid pandemic, the hospital still limited visitors to only one person a day. Lots of lovely friends asked if they could visit but I relied so much on Andy and simply wasn't prepared to sacrifice seeing him, with all his help for the day in order to see a friend. Visits from Claire were a definite bonus and although they always play it down, both her and Damian provided huge help and relief.

During this second stay, there was far more noise disturbance in that particular bay, it was very distressing, as it mostly came in the form of shouting, screaming and crying from another poor patient who happened to be in the bed opposite me.

Andy hired a wheelchair from a local business to enable me to escape from the ward. Even with the chair it was difficult because I had to wheel around my "feed bag" which had to be fed through a pump to get the thicker consistency into my body. The bag itself was 2kg and had to be suspended high from a drip stand which made it top heavy and unstable. This became very obvious in the middle of a night trip to the toilet, attempting to push the thing across the bay to the bathroom and hitting a slightly uneven part of flooring. The stand toppled over pulling everything with it. The tube from it was fed through my upper arm, under my armpit and into the large veins to my heart. When you are this connected to a weight that is about to crash to the floor, you really do not want all those tubes being ripped out. My automatic reaction was to grab at the stand and catch it, which amazingly I did, as it was halfway down. Being as I was not supposed to be lifting anything at all, the effort and weight of that catch was really not good and resulted in a considerable amount of pain immediately afterwards. Thankfully, after a visit from a doctor who happened to be passing through the ward, we agreed there seemed to be no harm done, but lesson learnt. I was so, so cautious pushing that thing around after that experience.

After a further two weeks of being confined to the ward I was incredibly grateful to see that rented wheelchair even though I also hated it.

The feed on the PICC line was eventually switched to a quicker rate meaning I could receive the calories at night and be free from the stand, bag and tubes during the day, this alone created a feeling of immense freedom and relief.

I used the wheelchair as a walking frame and when I couldn't walk any more, Andy would push me in the chair. (Initially walking around a hundred meters and then up to a quarter of a mile round the hospital corridors). Gradually we progressed and Andy would push me in the chair, taking me for some much needed fresh air. I would sit in the wheelchair, wrapped in a blanket and he would wheel me outside, we would sit in the peaceful sunshine and talk. The best of these visits were when Charlie came along too. As we were outside and off the ward it was fine to see more than one person and my Dad also came to visit. Charlie would hug me and hold my hand for the entire visit which was of course the best medicine of all.

During my time in the QE, (around two months in total) I lay terrified at night and praying, over and over again to God and to my Mum. I do feel both were with me in some way and I had some very vivid dreams about my dear Mum hugging me and bringing happiness. The reality was though, things kept going wrong and the praying to others didn't seem to help with this or with my fears. I couldn't stop being frightened – frightened of the cancer coming straight back, frightened of the infection not clearing and needing more surgery and frightened of not being around for my family. Finally, it dawned on me that any strength to deal with this, had to come from within me and from me alone and only I could change my thoughts and fears.

Previous to this realisation there was one episode that will always stay with me. I was brought up as catholic so when entering the hospital this is what I noted as my religion. One day, when my infection was particularly bad and I lay violently shivering in a pool of sweat unable to eat or drink, a priest pulled back the curtain to announce he had come to see me. I did wonder If he had been called in to give me my last rites (a final blessing before we die). He soon put me at ease and asked if he could sit with me a little and pray. I'm afraid I don't remember his name but after talking for a while he held my hand and prayed for me. He said three different prayers and on the last one he asked for God to cleanse and purify my body and mind. As he spoke, I felt a wave of warmth, not heat, just pleasant warmth wash slowly over me, travelling from the top of my head to the tip of my toes. I immediately stopped shivering and stopped feeling cold. I felt immediately improved.

It shook me (in a good way) so much, I cried – I cried a lot on that ward – but at that moment, they were tears of amazement and relief.

There are lots of different opinions on what I felt but, in my mind, it was a miracle for sure.

Going back several years, when Charlie was poorly, I had a similar experience. When his bloods became very worrying, I visited the vicar who married Andy and I. We talked and I cried and prayed with Rob (the vicar) who was so kind with his time, explanations and opinions. We prayed together for some time. The very next day the hospital called with much better news and a way forward and gradually over the following months and years his blood levels all returned to normal and everything changed for the better.

It is completely understandable why people doubt religion with all the wars, violence and disease in the world but personally I found having some belief and giving in to it from time to time has helped me a great deal. I believe these experiences of immediate improvements to me and to Charlie some years before, were not just as a result of my belief, other factors were at play that cannot be explained. I do feel there is something else, certainly something spiritual that none of us can explain.

Despite this wonderful experience with the priest in hospital, I was still, at times incredibly frightened. Andy and Charlie have been truly amazing with their strength and positivity throughout my illness and recovery, which has helped enormously but the night times, lay on my own were often terrifying.

In recent years I have found I am not great at being on my own, and can have a tendency to catastrophise any problems and worry over every little thing. In my younger years I never had these feelings of dread, buying my own property at the age of twenty-one and enjoying living on my own. As I have grown older though, time on my own is something I have struggled with and more so than ever during my hospital stay.

Andy would leave the hospital at around 3:30pm. Traffic was always terrible heading out of Birmingham and he needed to be home for Charlie as well as all the other chores he was doing. He literally never stopped through the two months I was in hospital. I hated the time he left and the wait until 11am the next day when visiting hours started and he was allowed back on the ward. He would always be there at 11 o'clock or before, waiting to be allowed through to me. I would be clock watching until he arrived and felt a huge sense of relief when he walked through that door. It became a source of amusement as the other ladies befriended him asking him to bring another blanket or fetch them a drink. I don't think I was the only one who looked forward to his visits. The dread would start again as 3:30pm approached and I knew I would be alone with my thoughts for the next eighteen or so hours.

Eventually I realised that all the praying in the world would not resolve anything without some input from myself. It took me a long time to come to this conclusion, I wish I had got there sooner! I had to become more self-sufficient in my thinking and certainly had to change my thought process.

During this time people were so kind, sending and recommending positive help books and similar. So many of these books related to the authors own hard times such as "Not getting the job I had interviewed for" or "A boyfriend finishing a relationship". These 'hard times' just seemed so trivial and really annoyed me.

I said to Andy "Surely these things are normal life situations, how can that qualify people to write self-help books on positive thinking methods?" It seemed very strange and my annoyance as to the irrelevance of their problems meant that I did not allow these self-help techniques to work for me.

For me, any form of calm wasn't going to come from reading these books either.

Eventually becoming quite cross with myself (which was probably what was needed), I made a list of all the good news relating to my health I could think of at that time. Although only relevant for me, a similar approach could help others in dealing with difficult situations. Finding without writing the "good stuff" down I would forget the good and return to focus on the bad. I wanted to stop that self-torment so every time that process started, out came my list.

My list was as follows:

1. The surgeon has cut out all the cancer. It's gone and he got clear margins so it's WELL gone.

2. So far it doesn't look like it has spread.

3. There is a 30% chance of it coming back but that's a much higher chance that it will NOT.

4. I will be scanned regularly after leaving hospital.

5. If it comes back, it will be caught sooner, will be smaller and can be cut out again.

6. If it hasn't come back in two years my odds have improved and then again after five years and again after ten.

7. The cancer experience is different for everyone so do not listen to horror stories (there were lots of these in the hospital and I didn't want to hear them and relate them back to myself).

8. Lance Armstrong is a well-known positive story as far as cancer and racing goes. He is well and still races now.

9. My fitness will help me recover from this experience.

So, I had NINE pieces of good news to focus on, and if I did that successfully, this would influence how I could view the future. I then made another list about how my pre-cancer lifestyle could influence my recovery now and in my future life.

My second list was drawn up, things to tell myself:

1. Think of the strength used in mind and body on long, cold, wet bike rides. You regularly rode 200kms in tough conditions and on these rides had 3-4 times when you felt great and 3-4 times when you felt awful but you always knew these awful times would end,

nd you would soon feel good again – use the same to get through these times in hospital.

2. This is just a blip in life. This is not how your life will be now, it's all just on hold. This was from one of the amazing nurses, Dan. It was just what I needed to hear at that particular time, but he didn't say it to pacify me, he genuinely meant and believed it and that's what made such a positive impact on me.

3. Stop living in fear. If you live like that you would never do anything, particularly on the bike and racing.

4. Life experiences can either break you or make you, which one do you want this to be.

5. Do you enjoy being frightened and worried? Does it serve any purpose at all?

6. Fear and worry will not help with a single thing. So why do it? You create the fear and worry so you can stop it. So stop!

With this need to control things more in mind, I then retrieved my Ironman notebook that was previously used for Ironman UK 2022, to make notes of the hotel, transitions, post codes etc.

The blue book was still in my overnight bag from the race. The bag had quickly become my hospital bag. Retrieving the book, I turned to a blank page and simply changed the book into my hospital note pad.

Oh dear! The poor surgeons must have dreaded coming to see me and the nurses must have thought I was a total pain. That dreaded blue book!!

With the help of nurse Dan, we made a list of all my medications, what they were, what they were for and what time they should be administered. Then each night, if I was worried about anything I would write it down so I could remember to ask Fabio the next day. Any important information the nurses gave me through the day I would write it down. Any decisions made; I wrote them down. Any changes at all I would write it all down. I kept a note of my temperature daily and my blood test results which were also taken every day. By doing all this, it was possible to monitor and see, slowly but surely there was a definite improvement which gave me comfort and huge relief to Andy.

In short, I had applied my obsession over the numbers in my fitness training to my cancer recovery, and because that was second nature to me, I felt for the first time that I was beginning to control my cancer journey rather than it controlling me.

My scar the week after surgery. 41cm from breast bone to public bone.

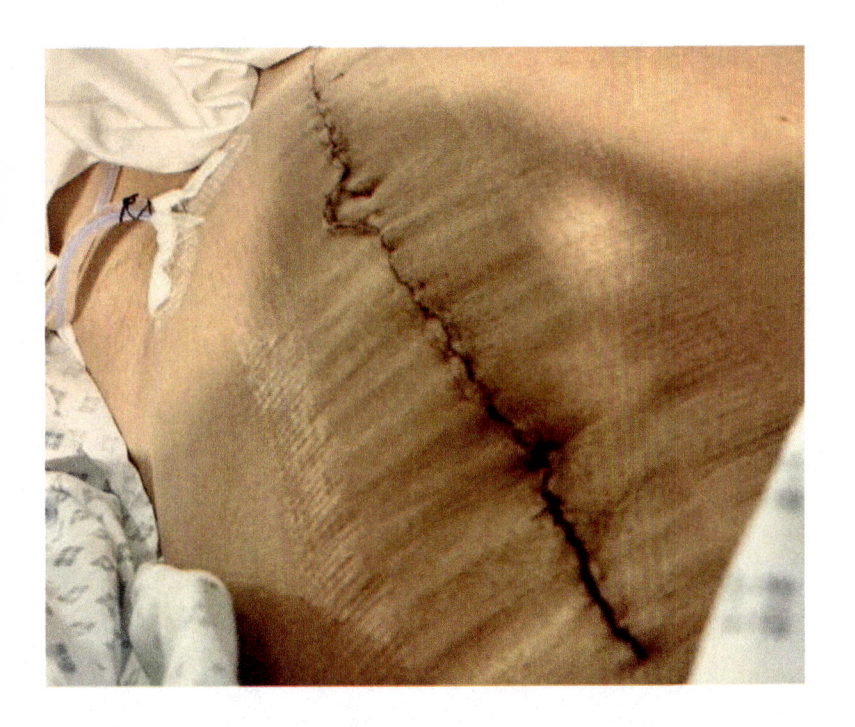

My first attempt at being home, before bouncing straight back and before I lost a lot more weight. Holding a 5KG medicine ball – the same weight as what was removed.

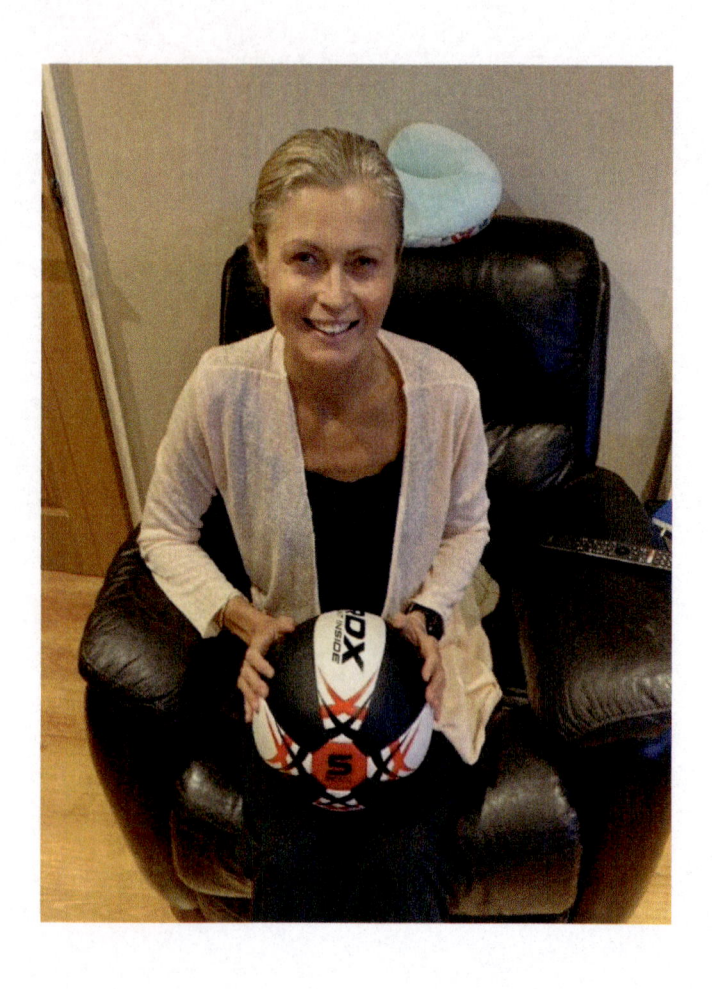

CHAPTER 9. There is no place like home

Thankfully over the next four weeks in the QE, my temperature became stable and I started to feel a little better. Once my feed line was switched to one with a quicker dispense rate, I could take on all the calories through the night and be free of the drip stand for Andy's visits.

It was such a relief in the hours I was free from those tubes and the awkward, unstable drip stand. It gave me a huge sense of freedom and I would put my Garmin watch on and walk the corridors, marking the time and distance compared to previous days. I was still hunched over and in pain but each day I managed to walk a little further and a little less hunched. Even if I only walked an extra ten metres, it was still a victory. We would still use the wheel chair as a walking frame and then, when I couldn't manage any more, I would move to the chair and Andy would push me. In this way, free from tubes, we managed to get outside the hospital into the hospital grounds and enjoy the fresh air which was definitely wonderful medicine.

The next stage in my recovery was for me to drink a milky hot drink. I was allowed a coffee! I love, love coffee!

After four weeks of nil by mouth it tasted SO good, even better than I remembered. After several more days of this and nights still attached to the PICC line, I was at last allowed to eat hospital food from a "low residual diet". Many people complain about hospital food but even that tasted pretty wonderful after not eating for so long. Mashed potatoes and gravy and no reaction. This was winning for me right now, not standing on a podium. These wins were more exciting than racing, as they were all steps closer to heading home.

I was closely monitored to see if there was any reaction from eating low residual foods and was still having to wear my drain which had syphoned off most of the infection aided by huge doses of IV antibiotics. The infection was still draining but the antibiotics seemed to have worked their magic and I had been off them for a couple of days, and even with eating, there was no sign of a temperature or another infection.

As the normal routine of the hospital day started – lights on, blood pressure and stats, blood test, breakfast (yay!), visit from the Sarcoma team. It was Mr Max Almond who visited as Fabio was not around on this particular day.

Mr Almond asked "Would you like to go home?"

"What? When?"

"Today"

I was perhaps a bit too passionate in my response "OH THANK GOD. YES PLEASE!"

The feeling of relief was overwhelming and this time when we left, I didn't feel half as stressed as the first time, more confident that I was well enough to return home.

The drain needed to stay in place, with the tube inserted through my back, into my abdominal cavity to drain any remaining infection. The bag into which it drained was then strapped to my leg. Various medication was given to me in a huge carrier bag to take home. Additionally, a daily injection was required, which Andy administered for me so we were given several weeks' worth of those. I didn't mind any of this and I couldn't wait for the comfort of home.

We deliberately had not told Charlie I was coming home as there had been so many setbacks and disappointments in the days and weeks before. We did not want to get his hopes up just to let him down again. After each one he became more and more despondent.

After arriving home and feeling wonderfully relaxed but also desperate to see my boy, I was excited to realise school had finished for the day and Charlie would soon be home. Before he arrived home from school I decided to hide. As soon as he walked through the door, I popped my head round from where I had been hiding. His face was a picture of joy. We all just stood and hugged each other and more than a few tears were shed.

The date was 15th November and it was so amazing to be home. Oh, the peace! There had been just so much noise in hospital, through both the day and night. The peace and quiet was wonderful. My own bed with warm soft sheets which covered a bed that was not hard plastic beneath. The shower, clean and easily controlled and no worry of someone else waiting to use the room. Our recliner chair that I could keep easily shifting my body through a range of movements when I became uncomfortable. Best of all Andy and Charlie both with me, making a fuss of me and not allowing me to lift a finger. It really was wonderful to be home.

The very next day Andy and I went for a trip out. We drove 15 minutes to a lake with a balcony café. We took a very short walk from the car park around the lake and enjoyed a delicious coffee on the balcony, in the sunshine. Just heavenly.

The following day we walked a mile and a half around another small lake with plenty of benches in case I needed to rest. But those benches were not needed, and even though I was struggling by the end, a lap of the lake was completed. It wasn't long before we started to build up the distances walked.

One afternoon Charlie and I went for a walk. He held my hand – (actually in public) but it was quiet so he was safely inconspicuous. He said to me cautiously "Mum. Do you think you will race again one day?"

I answered, "I don't know Charlie and I honestly don't care, so long as that thing never comes back."

Charlies' response was "Well if you ever get the chance to race Ironman again you should do it. Do you not think you would have been first instead of second if you hadn't been carrying five kilograms of cancer around with you?"

It made me laugh – and then think some.

As the walking became more comfortable, I was very fortunate to have some wonderful friends who would all come and walk with me at different times. Phil (my bike buddy) walked a few times with me around a local golf course, Jo (Pross. My best friend from school), Kate, Rachel and Jackie all walked this route which was fabulous for both my physical and mental rehabilitation.

Jackie is the wife of Elliott Nash. They are both incredibly kind people and Elliott has given me so much help in the form of sponsorship for my racing, through his business Elliott Nash Ltd. There are many races I couldn't have competed in without his help. Triathlon is not a cheap sport unfortunately.

They were both also incredibly supportive through my illness and so kind. Jackie would ask Andy to come with Charlie and join her and Elliott for dinner when I was in hospital. When I returned home, Jackie told me I looked really well, and then a while later confessed, "I was just being a friend... you looked dreadful!" We laughed a lot particularly as by then I had put on weight. It really didn't take me long at all to put on all the weight I had lost in hospital. I do like my food.

As for Elliott - he employs a number of people and cares about them all. He is a clever business man and very much believes in helping others. He sponsors a number of local sports people and teams, but he doesn't talk about it, he just enjoys helping.

After being home for a couple of months, Elliott visited us and said he would still like the same sponsorship deal for me throughout 2023, even though it was clear I wouldn't be able to race any time that year, if ever. I couldn't believe his generosity and kindness. He said, "There is no rush to race, absolutely do not try to rush back or let this put pressure on you but I would like to do that for you."

It was as always, a huge help, particularly after so many months being unable to work and I would love to do him proud one day if I get the chance.

The lovely messages received from friends in hospital helped keep me going while confined there and they didn't stop now I was home. They lifted me during the tougher days when the pain was more intense or I was having a worry.

Andy had a lot of support from his side of the family too who would all ask, almost daily how we all were and if we needed anything. In particular Nigel and Sharon who also live close were very supportive. They are such positive people; it has a positive effect on us all too.

Just a big thank you to everyone who supported us, it meant the world and still does.

When I was well enough, there were so many more lunches and dinners out than we are used to. It was just so good to see everyone and happily some of those arrangements have become regular routines.

On the 12th December I had my first check-up back at the QE hospital. I had been sent home on the 15th November with a drain still inserted in my back through into my abdominal cavity where the infection had been. It drained any last infection that may still be there and I still had to follow a low residual diet and just hope that the internals all repaired this time round.

I didn't want to do too much with this drain in, it was uncomfortable where it was inserted, the bag had to be strapped to my leg and it affected what clothes I could wear. It was another huge relief when Fabio was happy to have it removed at that December appointment. He was thrilled with my progress and we discussed activity levels and future scans. The drain came out, another step to recovering.

Additional improvement signs were coming off all medication and pain relief and stopping the injection which Andy had to administer for me each day. I registered each change in my blue book and I had to admit, the improvements were now accelerating and each felt like a giant step forward.

By 24th December we managed a five-mile hilly walk around the Lickey Hills near to where we live. There was such a heavy frost it looked like snow. So beautiful. Excitingly that week I also manged to sit on my bike on the indoor trainer and complete a twenty-minute easy spin.

"Well?" Asked Andy.

"It's absolutely fine" I giggled.

It felt so good and I noticed out the corner of my eye Andy trying (unsuccessfully) to hide a few tears of joy.

First morning home

December 27th Chipping Campden – NOT on the bike for a change

Following another couple of months to allow the huge scar and several smaller ones to repair further, I eventually started back cycling outside and swimming in the local pool. Building up very gradually with the help of Phil and the Beacon cycling guys.

To date, in addition to many miles on the bike, I have completed six century rides (100 miles or just over). The first one of these I completed in June 2023, having only ventured back out on my bike in March. Through the years of Ironman training, I have completed many of these longer rides but the one in June 2023 felt extra special and gave me a buzz like I have never experienced before from cycling. I walked in the house like I had won the Tour de France.

Andy and I have enjoyed lots of walking but as expected, I have not yet been able to return to my beloved running, not with any consistency anyway. A little frustratingly, every time I try to introduce my favourite sport, even as a slow jog, I experience some level of pain and discomfort.

After so long spent as bed rest and then the months relying on short walks, returning to running is clearly going to take some considerable time. Re-activating all those wasted muscles and putting that jarring through the body.

I will keep trying and meanwhile am enjoying my cycling and swimming immensely.

The advice given, back on discharge day was to expect around twelve months to walk pain free from this huge operation. So honestly, to be able to swim and cycle is a huge privilege and I will never be able to thank the surgery team enough for what they have given me.

Although most people understand me, I have actually been asked why I am doing all this activity after what I have been through. Well, why wouldn't I?! It's what I love doing. The other option is to have more time to sit around worrying. No thanks.

In January I managed to start seeing a few clients back in clinic for sports massage. It's such a physical job I needed to keep the numbers low initially and gradually build back, as I would my training. Returning to work was another milestone for me, not only for the sense of improvement it gave me, but for the normality of life returning. I knew straightaway that I still loved to hear about everyone's training and racing plans for the summer ahead and wanted to keep them on track.

My life for now involves scans and check-ups at the Queen Elizabeth hospital, initially every three months but that has now changed to every six. There are good days when I feel positive and blessed to be alive and some bad days when I feel frightened or just sad for what I have been through and put my family through. When I feel like this I look back on my positive notes from the hospital or catch up with positive friends.

Some people always know exactly what to say and never fail to make me feel better. I have even had a hug from my Dad!

I can honestly say, so long as "THAT THING" never comes back, I'll be happy, even if I never race again.

Although….It wouldn't be a bad end to this story would it?!

Printed in Great Britain
by Amazon